Also by Rev. Curry Pikkaart

TNT (Tempted, Nurtured, & Triumphant), a small-group discipleship resource coproduced with his wife, Barbara.

7 Habits of Highly Healthy People (Antidotes for the 7 Deadly Sins), Maitland: Xulon Press, 2007.

For more information and inspiration visit www.pastorcurry.com

When the Going Gets Tough...

Turn Your Stumbling Blocks Into Stepping Stones

REV. CURRY PIKKAART

WESTBOW
PRESS®
A DIVISION OF THOMAS NELSON
& ZONDERVAN

WestBow Press books may be ordered through booksellers or by contacting:

WestBow Press
A Division of Thomas Nelson & Zondervan
1663 Liberty Drive
Bloomington, IN 47403
www.westbowpress.com
1 (866) 928-1240

ISBN: 978-1-5127-5079-9 (sc)
ISBN: 978-1-5127-5080-5 (hc)
ISBN: 978-1-5127-5078-2 (e)

Library of Congress Control Number: 2016911908

Print information available on the last page.

WestBow Press rev. date: 07/29/2016

Dedication

With love and overwhelming gratitude, I dedicate this book to

John and Jewel Pikkaart
my dear departed parents, whose love, discipline, support and commitment to Jesus Christ led me to Jesus Christ and ultimately to accepting His call on me to be a minister of the gospel. My only regret is that this is a post-mortem dedication they are not here to read. However, I believe they will somehow see it.

Shirley Toering
My beloved sister, who, like my parents, has never wavered in her faith and has consistently demonstrated how to navigate rough waters of life's journey. Still today, you inspire me. Thank you for your love, example, and faith.

True followers of Jesus are absurdly happy, totally fearless, and almost always in trouble.
—Meister Eckhart

Contents

Preface

I'm filled with gratitude for the abundant blessings poured into my life. God is good, but I believe my life is not that spectacular or unusual, probably not much different from yours. I'm just an average person who has tried to live in step with Jesus. My life is rich, but it hasn't always been easy. Sometimes, I made good choices, but at other times, I didn't. Sometimes, my road has been level, but at times, it's been mountainous.

Through the years, I've observed that this is pretty much the norm for most people. I don't know anyone who can claim he or she has lived without tough times, which are simply part of life. This is why I'm so drawn to Joseph and his story in Genesis. I've always been fascinated because throughout his life, he'd take one step forward and two steps back, and I can identify with that. Yet in his journey and his relationship with God, he always moved onward and upward. I want also to identify with that.

So throughout my forty-plus years of ministry, I've read and reread, studied, preached, and taught Joseph's story. While doing so, it's been my privilege to share in thousands of people's life journeys as they too have entered tough times and seasons. Each of them had to decide how to approach them. Some were defeated by them, some embraced them, but none escaped them. One constant for me was the story of Joseph, which always had something to offer.

Many others have written about Joseph's life, some very eloquently and powerfully. I'm not trying to better them because I cannot. I merely desire the help of the Holy Spirit in sharing how Joseph and his God have affected my heart and strengthened my unspectacular, average life. In doing so, I hope and pray that whether your tough times are in the past, present, or future, you can see yourself in Joseph's story, in God's story, and be impacted and strengthened as well.

I pray that you will be able to identify the tough times in your life and then come to see them as stumbling blocks that can be turned into stepping stones. I pray above all else that you will enter into a deeper relationship with Jesus Christ. To Him be all the glory!

Acknowledgments

A special thank you to my editor from WestBow Press, Martin McHugh. Focusing on the oral act of preaching for over 40 years, it's difficult to write my thoughts in a smooth readable style and format. Without your assistance the readability of this book would be greatly diminished. I've learned a great deal from, and been blessed by you.

I could fill numerous pages with other acknowledgements since this book is the product of sixty-seven years of living. I have learned life lessons from so many people that to name them all would be a massive undertaking, and even then I'd miss some. I apologize to those I've missed and offer my thanks for the roles they played in my life. But here's my best effort to acknowledge those most responsible for their impact on this book.

I begin with all who were members of Bethany Reformed Church in Kalamazoo, Michigan, between 1949 and 1974 (birth to ordination). I thank them all for their nurture, love, and guidance during the critical formative years of my life. You witnessed and contributed to my baptism, my profession of faith, and my ordination. I realize now how powerfully you modeled not just living in but moving through tough times.

I am deeply indebted to all the congregations with whom it was a privilege to share in ministry: First Reformed Church of Sioux Center, Iowa; First Reformed Church of Holland, Michigan; Trinity Reformed Church of Kalamazoo, Michigan; Bethany Reformed and Orchard Hill Churches in Grand Rapids, Michigan; and Hope Reformed Church in South Haven, Michigan. You have patiently listened to my teaching and preaching on the themes of this book, have opened up your lives to me, and loved, encouraged, and supported my family through the years. While we experienced so much joy, we also shared tough times together. I never failed to learn from you.

I've been blessed to have worked with wonderful staff in all those congregations, and to you, I give heartfelt thanks. You were always my inner circle and my special family as we shared so much of life and ministry together—sorrows and joys, tough and good times. Your partnership in the gospel means more to me than I can express.

It was an honor and joy to serve with Tom Bos for many years. Tom, you were more than a cohort and peer; you were and still are a dear friend who served as a pastor to me even as I attempted to pastor others. I wouldn't trade our time together for anything. I have so much for which to be thankful, but there were many moments I wasn't sure I'd make it through. You were always there to comfort, counsel, guide, and strengthen me. Never once did you walk away. You've been a priceless gift. Thank you, and may our Lord bless you.

Larry DeBruyne, has anyone ever had such a loyal, wise, perceptive, caring friend as I have had in you? You were always there at just the right time in just the right way with just the right words and presence. You were often there not because you knew something was up but because the Spirit led you there when something *was* up. With you, I could be me with total transparency, a rare gift. So many tough times walked through, so many lessons learned from you, so much love received from you. Because of you, I look back on my life and see very few stumbling blocks but a lot of stepping stones, many of which have a tribute to you on them. May you too be blessed by Jesus.

I thank and praise God for my precious wife. Barb, without your undying love for and support of me, this book would never have been written. Your constant encouragement kept me at the task. You've sacrificed much through our years of ministry and now through my time of writing, but you never wavered. Your love and prayers fueled my passion especially at times when it would otherwise have waned. We have shared so much joy and so many blessings even in the many tough times because you have helped me remain focused on and faithful to Jesus. I look forward to these years of "retirement" when we can share even more time together. I join our boys in rising up and calling you blessed.

Speaking of our boys, I'm reminded of the psalmist who wrote, "Children are a gift from the LORD; they are a real blessing" (Psalm 127:3 GNT). Brad, Brian, and Kevin, you have no idea how much you've blessed and enriched my life. Far too often, especially in the early years of my ministry, I gave more attention to the church than I did to you. The tough times of life and ministry affected you as well; we shared many of them. Yet you loved me. You didn't turn into haters of the church or me or rebel against the church or me. Instead, you and your mother always loved me with the love of Christ. Were it not for that, I wouldn't have written this book. Thank you. I'm so grateful to God for His faithfulness through you.

Most of all, I give thanks to Jesus Christ. Without Him, my life would be a different story; I'd have little if anything worth writing about. Without Him, my tough times would have been stumbling blocks; with Him, they were stepping stones to a deeper relationship with Him. Thank You, Jesus. May all the glory go to You.

Introduction

Some people see Joseph as a spoiled brat who loved to lord it over his brothers and pretty much got what he deserved. Some see him as a wise, determined young man who decided to do everything he could to end his family's sad history of deception and dysfunction. Some see him simply as an innocent victim of the twists and turns of life.

While it can be fun to debate which was the case, there's a greater issue. How did Joseph see the events in his life? Did his circumstances happen by chance or by choice? Did they happen merely by chance so all Joseph could do was make the best of them? Or did they happen by his choice, or God's choice, or both?

Do our choices and God's choices somehow work in partnership to move us through the tough times into the next chapter of our life story? Is what happens *to* us meant to affect what happens *in* us? Are our life events invitations from God to enter a partnership with Him? Could everything that is said to us and happens to and around us be invitations from God to let His glory and presence shine where we are? Could God long to be known in and through us in everything?

You choose how to answer. May Joseph's life speak to you.

CHAPTER 1

When the Going Gets Tough …
Dreams Become Pathways

Genesis 37:1–36

Joseph's brothers putting Joseph into the pit

Dream: an involuntary occurring to one awake; an aspiration, goal, aim.

It was a great time for the dream. It was happening in other places, and it could happen in our community as well. So our group developed an exciting vision for establishing a Christian nightclub, a restaurant/cafe where Christian artists would sing as people dined and relaxed. We had some influential people on the committee, had some good contacts, had prayed diligently, had gained great support, and had a place to purchase. It was all systems go. But nothing ever developed. Things never got beyond our meetings. The dream never got off the ground. The trouble with dreams is that sometimes they don't work out as planned.

I remember beginning a ministry in a church as the pastor of education and youth. At the time the youth program was all but nonexistent. Parents seemed excited about my coming; they promised their kids would be faithful in attendance. The kids said they were enthused. So my wife and I set a date for a get-acquainted party, bought the goodies, planned the games and schedule, sent out the personal invitations, and prayed while waiting for the night to arrive. The night arrived. Two youths showed up. The trouble with dreams is that sometimes they don't work out as planned.

Annette and her husband were glad to be missionaries in Western Europe, but she developed severe back pain, and X-rays revealed a grapefruit-sized tumor on her spinal cord. Since it was relatively routine and not particularly high risk, she underwent surgery. But when she woke up, she was paralyzed from the neck down and in even worse excruciating and constant pain. Shortly thereafter, Annette and her husband and five children moved back to the United States, where she could be cared for in more-appropriate surroundings.[1] The trouble with dreams is that sometimes they don't work out as planned.

I have a hunch you know what I'm talking about. Ever seen your dreams collapse, your road filled with detours, your best-laid plans fall flat? How did you feel? Where did you turn? What did you do? Who could have helped? I've found the best place to turn is to God's Word, where we find God working in the lives of people whose experiences match ours. We can learn what to do from their experiences when the going gets tough and our dreams collapse.

Joseph's story begins in Genesis 37. The scene (vv. 1–11) is filled with dreams and plans. Young Joseph (around seventeen or so) had been given a royal robe by his father and had received two significant dreams from God. He knew God had a special plan for him to become a great leader. The dream marked him as God's person. So throughout his life, Joseph focused on his life's purpose. He didn't know all the details, but he didn't need to. The knowledge at that point was enough. It propelled him through many of the turbulent waters through which he would eventually swim. It gave him a sense of divine destiny and the knowledge he would be used by God.

When our best-laid plans don't work out, we too should focus on the purpose for our lives. A sense of purpose, of divine destiny, is critical for life. In the difficult times of life, it can sustain and embolden us and give us strength; it can infuse us with energy to stay the course. I want to be clear here—a sense of purpose and destiny will not give us a way out of our tough times; rather, they give us a pathway around, through, or over the obstacles threatening our journey. Purpose and destiny are two of the most powerful motivating forces of life.

Even agnostic author Charles Murray, in an interview regarding culture and human achievement, acknowledged the power of purpose.

> A major stream of human accomplishment is fostered by a culture in which the most talented people believe that life has a purpose and that the function of life is to fulfill that purpose ... It is harder for an agnostic or an atheist than a Christian to find purpose, because a devotion to a human cause, whether social justice, the environment, the search for truth, or an abstract humanism, is by its nature less compelling than devotion to God. Here, Christianity has its most potent advantage. The incentives of forgiveness of sin and eternal life are just about as powerful as incentives get. The nonbeliever has to make do with comparatively tepid alternatives.[2]

Make no mistake—the good news is that there is a divine purpose for your life. God has a plan and purpose for you. At your baptism, at your profession of faith, or in the quiet prayer of commitment you offered when the Spirit of God drew you to Him, God heard your testimony, dreams, and promises, but even more important, He claimed you and marked you as His own. As the late Horace Bushnell put it,

> God has a definite plan for every human person, girding him, visibly or invisibly, for some exact thing, which it will be the true significance and glory of his life to have accomplished.

Many persons, I am well aware, never even think of any such thing. They suppose that, for most, life is a necessarily stale and common affair. What it means for them they do not know, and they scarcely conceive that it means anything. They even complain … that while some few are set forward by God to do great works and fill important places, they are not allowed to believe that there is any particular object in their existence … The Holy Scriptures never give way to this … but hold up the dignity of common life, and giving meaning to its appointments.[3]

In 1982, Nick Vujicic was born with tetra-amelia syndrome, a rare genetic disorder. Nick has no arms or legs, just two small feet attached to his torso. Nick struggled emotionally and physically to accept his condition as he was growing up. But today, as a follower of Christ, Nick has what he calls "a ridiculously good life." Nick wrote,

When I'm asked how I can claim a ridiculously good life when I have no arms or legs, [people] assume I'm suffering from what I lack. They inspect my body and wonder how I could possibly give my life to God, who allowed me to be born without limbs. Others have attempted to soothe me by saying that God has all the answers and then when I'm in heaven I will find out his intentions. Instead, I choose to live by what the Bible says, which is that God is the answer today, yesterday, and always.

When people read about my life or witness me living it, they are prone to congratulate me for being victorious over my disabilities. I tell them that my victory came in surrender. It comes every day when I acknowledge that I can't do this on my own, so I say to God, "I give it to you!" Once I yielded, the Lord took my pain and turned it into something good … He gave my life meaning when no one and nothing else could provide it. [And] if God can take someone like me, someone without arms and legs, and use me as his hands and feet, he can use anybody. It's not about ability. The only thing God needs from you is a willing heart.[4]

Do you have a willing heart? What motivates, captures, and drives you? The call of God on your life? A sense of divine calling and purpose that God will use you? Are you listening to Him as He leads you through life? Do your dreams and best-laid plans include God?

Perhaps you want to live out God's purpose for your life but are unsure of your specific purpose. Jesus gave us all a purpose for living whether or not we know it. Jesus said, "You did not choose me but I chose you and appointed you to go and bear fruit—fruit that will last" (John 15:16). God has a purpose for your life. He wants you to bear fruit in all you do. You may not know the particulars now of your unique purpose; that's okay. Just bear fruit until it becomes clear.

Have you sensed God's unique purpose for you? Does it challenge and stretch you? Are you true to it? Have you committed your way and your life to Christ so He can lead you further along His path? If your answer is "Yes", continue listening to God through His Word, in worship, and with prayer.

If you haven't yet grasped your unique purpose, pray for God to remove the scales from your eyes and heart so you can see and hear Him. Living without a purpose is like trying to navigate a canoe without a paddle or drive a car with no gas. Dreams can become pathways to navigate life and stay on course, God's course. Dreams can become the fuel that empowers you to keep driving toward God's destination.

When plans don't work out, focus on the purpose of life, but be aware of the path of obstacles (vv. 15–35). Someone aptly said, "We dream in the world in which we live, but the world in which we live is not a dream world." Life is filled with obstacles and hard times. They jump on us the moment we leave our mothers' wombs. Actions and decisions of other people impact the pursuit of our purpose. So do accidents, tragedies, illnesses, and a host of other unplanned, unpredictable circumstances. Joseph said a simple good-bye to his father, Jacob, left for a short journey to see his brothers, and it was twenty-two years before he and his father said hello again. Neither Jacob nor Joseph recognized that Joseph's dreams had become his brother's nightmares. And their treatment of Joseph was only the first of many obstacles and trials that made Joseph's going tough. In addition to being dumped in that pit, he spent time as a slave and as a prisoner, experienced temptation from an officer's wife, and ultimately was exposed to all the trappings of wealth and power. He faced obstacles that challenged his body, soul, mind, faith, and attitude. He was constantly confronted with reexamining his purpose and had to ask if it was true.

We too are at times confronted with questioning or reexamining our purpose. In my denomination, every seminary student must be under the care of what we call a classis, a group of churches in a specified geographic area. As a senior in college, I entered their care. The chairperson of their Student Care Committee told me, "Just be sure and let us know how we can help. We're ready to support you in anyway, financially or whatever!" That was for me one more affirmation God wanted me in seminary.

Later, when I went to the committee and asked for financial assistance, I was told, "We don't have any funds for that. Sorry!" An obstacle. To top it off, I couldn't get any aid from the seminary because even though it was a graduate school, my father's salary was used as a basis to determine financial need. So there I was with a wife, an infant, no full-time job, and no financial assistance. It was easy for me to wonder if indeed this was God's purpose for me.

You've faced your share of obstacles as well. Whenever you try to live out God's purpose, you'll meet obstacles. As you can learn from Joseph, the key is to resolve to do two things. First, be willing to see each obstacle as an opportunity to acquire knowledge and experience; be willing to patiently learn from them. Learn that many people won't understand your sense of purpose; learn that many others will try to block you or mock you; learn that sometimes life deals you a bad hand. President Dwight Eisenhower once shared a powerful learning of his boyhood years.

> My brothers and I were playing a game with my mother. The game was with cards—not regular playing cards because she was too straight laced for that—but a hand was dealt and I remember this night mother dealt me an utterly impossible hand. And I began to complain about it. She said, "Boys, put your cards down. I want to tell you something, especially you, Dwight. You are playing a game in your home with your

mother under loving circumstances. We all love each other here and I have dealt you a bad hand. Now when you get out in life where they don't love you so much, you are going to be dealt many a bad hand. What are you to do? You are to pray to God. You are to trust God and like a man you are to play the hand that is dealt you." "And that," said Eisenhower, "is one of the wisest things I learned in my youth."[5]

Resolve to patiently learn.

Second, resolve to persevere. Stand by your purpose and dream; let it drive you. One of my favorite sayings is, "Be led by dreams, not pushed by problems." Dreams aren't fulfilled overnight; purposes are not fully realized quickly. So turn your stumbling blocks into stepping stones. Plato wrote the first sentence of his famous *Republic* nine ways before he was satisfied. Cicero practiced speaking before friends every day for thirty years to perfect his elocution. Noah Webster labored thirty-six years on his dictionary, crossing the Atlantic twice to gather information. Milton rose at 4:00 a.m. every day to have enough hours to write *Paradise Lost*. As Charles Spurgeon once said, "By perseverance the snail reached the ark."[6]

A story is told that while building the Panama Canal, Col. George Washington Goethals had to contend with the many problems of geography and climate and the criticism of countless people back home who predicted he'd never complete the task, but he persevered. One day, a worker asked him, "Aren't you going to answer your critics?" "In time," he answered. "How?" asked the worker. Goethals smiled. "With the canal." When obstacles tempt you to question or forget your purpose and divine destiny, resolve to learn and persevere. Life is not a matter of chance but of choice; you seldom choose what happens to you, but you can choose how you respond. Choose the wise response; stick to your God-given purpose; be pushed by your God-given dreams.

When plans don't work, focus on the purpose of life and be aware of the path of obstacles. And the foundation of your focus should be the providence of God. You live by choices, God's and yours. You make choices that radically affect your life, and so does God. But amazingly, God doesn't violate or overrule your freedom; rather he uses your choices. "Meanwhile the Midianites sold Joseph in Egypt to Potiphar, one of

Pharaoh's officials, the captain of the guard" (v. 36). If you know the end of the story, you're aware that verse 36 means more than what is stated. God, through Joseph, would be victorious. In seeking to defeat God's purposes, the brothers actually advanced them. Joseph became a valued leader who eventually saved his family from famine and preserved the life of God's chosen people all because his brothers had sold him into slavery.

Just as Joseph and his brothers made their own choices, you make your own free choices in life, and God makes His. Without violating your freedom, He will have His way. Amazing, isn't it? As God proclaimed through the prophet Isaiah, "'My thoughts are not your thoughts, neither are my ways your ways,' declares the Lord. 'As the heavens are high above the earth, so are my ways higher than your ways and my thoughts than your thoughts.'" (Isaiah 55:8). The providence of God is real. You make choices and God makes choices; God uses both to influence the course of your life.

Imagine for a moment that you're on a cruise to a predetermined destination. Along the way, there may be some side trips and visits to harbors, but those were predetermined as well. While onboard, however, you can make choices every day—where and what to eat, what activities to engage in, where to wander on the ship and with whom, on and on— and the other passengers make choices as well. But none of those choices change your destination because the captain keeps the ship on the course for the predetermined destination.

Similarly your ultimate destination in life has been set. There are some side trips on the itinerary. Yet you make choices every day. God's sovereignty doesn't overrule your freedom, and your choices don't overrule God's sovereignty.

When your dreams hit snags, remember that things aren't always what they seem. A pastor visited an elderly woman in his congregation. As they chatted, he started eating peanuts from a bowl and absentmindedly ate them all. Embarrassed, he apologized for his impoliteness. The woman responded, "That's okay. With my teeth the way they are, whenever someone gives me a can of those, I just lick the chocolate off and toss the peanuts into the bowl." Things aren't always what they seem.

Certainly Joseph the dreamer's life was not what it seemed. He was betrayed by his brothers, sold into slavery, led to Egypt, separated from family against his will, and forced to be in a place he didn't want to be. He was first a slave and then a prisoner. His dream had hit a brick wall. Or had it?

It's important to remember God is always working things out so things aren't always what they seem. The darkest moments of life are often cloudy corridors leading to sunlit rooms where the light of God is brightly shining. Joseph's life became much more than slavery and imprisonment; he was on the path to fame and prosperity. Your frustrated plans are but pieces of God's quilt that will be completed only at the completion of your life. Joseph's problems weren't isolated incidents; they occurred in the fabric of everyday living yet were sown in the mind of God on the material of eternity. In their book *Tending to the Holy,* Bruce and Katherine Epperly put it nicely: "Our attentiveness to God, even in the smallest details of daily life, transforms our world from a series of unrelated events to a unified, albeit open-ended, holy adventure in which God guides and inspires every encounter."[7]

An ancient fable illustrates the way to look at dreams and plans that do not work out. A rabbi went on a journey with the prophet Elijah. They walked all day, and at nightfall, they came to the humble cottage of a poor man whose only treasure was a cow. The poor man and his wife ran out to welcome the strangers for the night and offer them simple hospitality. Elijah and the rabbi were entertained with plenty of cow's milk, sustained by homemade bread and butter, and slept in the only bed while their hosts lay before the fire. But in the morning, the poor man's cow was dead.

They walked all the next day and arrived at the house of a very wealthy merchant whose hospitality they craved. The merchant was rich, but he lodged them in a cowshed and fed them bread and water.

In the morning, however, Elijah thanked him very much for what he had done and as a return for his kindness, he sent a mason to fix a wall that needed repair. The rabbi was unable to keep his silence; he begged the holy man to explain the meaning of his dealings with humans.

> "In regards to the poor man who received us so hospitably," replied the prophet, "it was decreed that his wife was to die that night, but in reward for his goodness God took the cow instead of the wife. I repaired the wall of the rich miser because

a chest of gold was concealed near the place, and if the miser had repaired the wall himself he would have discovered the treasure. Say not therefore to the Lord, "What doest thou?" But say in thy heart: Must not the Lord of all do right?"

I mentioned Annette living at home, paralyzed from the neck down and in excruciating, constant pain. Several years after her return home, Scott Larson had the opportunity to visit Annette and her family in their home. In his own words, here is what he found.

What I encountered when I entered their home was a beautifully dressed woman whose outward expression revealed little of her physical pain. During my five-hour visit, Annette served as a gracious hostess who shared her story with honesty. She told how when she first came out of the surgery, she and everyone else focused on praying for God to heal her. When that didn't happen and she was confined to 24-hour care at home, she became very depressed. Most people stopped connecting with her. Their lives moved on while Annette's came to a screeching halt. Bible college and missionary training had not equipped her to deal with a life tied to a wheelchair and filled with constant pain.

"I felt that I was left with three choices," said Annette. "To kill myself and end the unbearable suffering for all of us; to abandon my faith in God and merely exist on painkillers; or to put my energies to discovering God in the midst of all of this suffering."

Annette's face beamed. "I chose the third," she said. "And as I began slowly reading the Bible again through the lens of pain and suffering, what I saw was a God who was familiar with both. I thought my pain and suffering had taken me to a place where God could never be found; instead, it was a place where he became more real to me than I had ever known him to be."[8]

Must not the Lord of all the earth do right?

So we leave Joseph here as a slave, but we know he will one day rule. Surely, he shared the testimony of the psalmist, "God drew me up out of the desolate pit … and set my feet upon a rock, making my steps secure" (Psalm 40:2 RSV). Remember Joseph and his dreams and plans; more important, remember Joseph's God. Remember He gave His Son Jesus to die for you. He offers you eternal life, forgiveness, love, and acceptance. God chooses to knit your life together for good; the Lord of all the earth will do right. Will you choose to travel the pathway of trusting Him?

For Your Reflection

> Be still, my soul: the Lord is on thy side.
> Bear patiently the cross of grief or pain.
> Leave to thy God to order and provide;
> In every change, He faithful will remain.
> Be still, my soul: thy best, thy heavenly friend
> Through thorny ways leads to a joyful end.
>
> Be still, my soul: thy God doth undertake
> To guide the future, as He has the past.
> Thy hope, thy confidence let nothing shake;
> All now mysterious shall be bright at last.
> Be still, my soul: the waves and winds still know
> His voice who ruled them while He dwelt below.
>
> Be still, my soul: the hour is hastening on
> When we shall be forever with the Lord.
> When disappointment, grief and fear are gone,
> Sorrow forgot, love's purest joys restored.
> Be still, my soul: when change and tears are past
> All safe and blessed we shall meet at last.[9]

CHAPTER 2

When the Going Gets Tough ... Pitfalls Become Launching Pads

Genesis 39:1–6

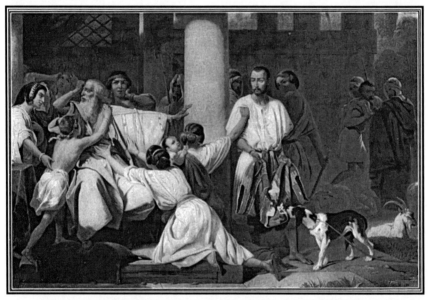

Joseph's brothers present his bloody coat to Jacob

Pitfall: a concealed pit prepared as a trap for men or animals; any trap or danger for the unwary.

My wife and I were alarmed as news broke that workers and staff at the Focus on the Family main office in Colorado were being held hostage by a gunman. *Who's the gunman? What does he want? Is this political retaliation?*

we wondered. Since one of our sons worked in another city for a sister organization of Focus, we were distressed. *Could they be next?*

Fortunately, the situation was relatively short lived and no one was physically harmed; many hostage situations don't turn out so well. But some released hostages offer inspiring testimonies about the faith that sustained them. Most of us feel far removed from such situations; we're sure that will never happen to us. Yet have you ever felt dumped into a pit with no way out? Boxed in? Stymied by what life has handed you? Unable to do anything constructive? Have you been held hostage in other ways? Have your circumstances ever gotten the better of you?

Joseph's life journey reminds us that when we're feeling trapped, when we're stuck in a pit, we should be more concerned about what we bring to life than what life brings to us. We need to get a faith grip and use the pit as a launching pad.

A faith grip helps bring an attitude adjustment to life. Consider Joseph, Jacob's youngest son. He had two grand dreams in which he saw his brothers and family bowing to him; since his father already showed favoritism to him, his brothers were jealous and despised Joseph.

One day, his father sent him to bring greetings and supplies to his brothers, who were in a distant field. But out of their spite, his brothers threw him into a pit to die. One brother, however, thought better of it, so they sold him into slavery. "Now Joseph had been taken down to Egypt. Potiphar, an Egyptian who was one of Pharaoh's officials, the captain of the guard, bought him from the Ishmaelites who had taken him there" (39:1). Joseph became a slave.

Imagine what it must have been like for this seventeen- or eighteen-year-old hitched to a camel, bound to people he didn't know, leaving behind his family and home, with no idea what the future held, and wondering, *Where is God? What's the future hold for me? What about my dreams?* He was a hostage, taken where he did not want to go, with a people he did not want to be with, in a situation he did not create. Talk about the going being tough.

When have you been a hostage held by a situation you didn't create, a situation beyond your control? An illness? A handicap? A job for which you weren't prepared? Or no job at all? Maybe you're being held hostage by the loss of a loved one or the pain of a shattered relationship. You cannot seem to move forward. Perhaps you feel captive in your marriage or family. Whatever your situation, you're in a circumstance in which you'd never put yourself, in a place you do not want to be.

When there is no apparent way out, you have a choice. You can sit and moan, gripe and complain. You can reminisce about how great life used to be and how unfair it now is. But fretting over what's lost or left behind only immobilizes you. Fighting, griping, and complaining only wastes energy. Like a horse in a halter, if you struggle too hard, you'll strangle yourself.

So what can you do? Like Joseph, you can apply a faith attitude and use your pitfall as a launching pad. Begin by accepting your current situation. Joseph accepted his. He was learning what an anonymous poet captured beautifully.

> We climbed the height by the zigzag path
> And wondered why—until
> We understood it was made zigzag
> To break the force of the hill.
>
> A road straight up would prove too steep
> For the traveler's feet to tread;
> The thought was kind in its wise design
> Of a zigzag path instead.
>
> It is often so in our daily life;
> We fail to understand
> That the twisting trail our feet must tread
> By love alone was planned.
>
> Then murmur not at the winding way,
> It is our Father's will
> To lead us home by the zigzag path,
> To break the force of the hill.

What about your zigzag paths? Can you identify some? Are you traveling one now? Can you accept it?

Joseph accepted his situation and did the best he could in it. He wasn't just an ordinary slave; he was a faithful, obedient slave. Later, he wasn't a common prisoner; he was a helpful, obedient prisoner. He wasn't any household manager; he was an extraordinarily loyal and responsible manager. He did what was required of him and then some.

On your zigzag paths, do what is required of you and then some. The parable of the pencil portrays the principal.

A pencil maker took a pencil aside just before putting him in a box. "There are five things you need to know," he told the pencil, "before I send you out in to the world. Always remember them and never forget, and you will become the best pencil you can be. "One: You'll be able to do many great things but only if you allow yourself to be held in someone's hand.

"Two: You'll experience a painful sharpening from time to time, but you need it to become a better pencil.

"Three: I will be able to correct mistakes you might make.

"Four: The most important part of you will always be what's inside.

"And Five: On every surface you are used on, you must leave your mark. No matter what the condition, you must continue to write."[10]

When the going gets tough, turn your pitfall into a launching pad. Keep writing your story. Your mind-set makes all the difference in the world.

Consider two paraplegics who appeared in the news about one week apart.[11] One was Kenneth Wright, a high school football star, an avid wrestler, boxer, hunter, and skin diver. In 1979, he sustained a broken neck in a wrestling match. He underwent therapy; the doctors were hopeful he would one day walk with braces and crutches. But at age twenty-four, he committed suicide.

The second paraplegic was Jim McGowan. At age nineteen, he was stabbed and was paralyzed from the middle of the chest down. He was confined to a wheelchair. Yet eventually, he made news by making a successful parachute jump into the middle of a target in the Pocono Mountains. He has lived alone, cooked his meals, washed his clothes, and cleaned his house. He drove a specially equipped automobile, wrote three books, and did the photography for America's first book on the history of wheelchair sports. He has since attempted to swim the English Channel.

Attitude and mind-set make a difference. As the legendary John Wooden wrote, "Things turn out best for those who make the best of the way things turn out."[12] No matter what, keep writing your story.

You might as well serve the best you can where you are because you cannot serve where you are not. Develop the mentality of a victor rather than a victim by doing your duty. I believe that's part of what Paul meant when he told us, "Continue to work out your salvation with fear and trembling, for it is God who works in you to will and to act in order to fulfill his good purpose" (Philippians 2:12–13). God is working in you, so even if you're in a pit, maximize your current opportunities for serving God. The helpful, productive question to ask is not "Why am I here?" but "How can I serve faithfully here?" As one writer put it poignantly,

> Why am I here and not in another part of the world?
> Why am I who I am and not a person of another race or belief?
> Why am I what I am instead of being in another occupation or social status?
> Because God appointed me to this time, this place, this name, this work.
> He gave me this body and this personality, this work to do and these things to do it with because he chose them best for me.
> If the choosing had been mine, I would always wonder if it had been right.
> Since God chose, all I need to do is put it to work![13]

Consider an adjustment of your attitude; accept your situation and do the best you can and then some. It will launch you further into God's plan for you.

In addition to making an attitude adjustment, getting a faith grip involves doing some asset accounting. Verses 2–6 show the impact of Joseph's presence and life on others because of Joseph's attitude.

> The Lord was with Joseph so that he prospered, and he lived in the house of his Egyptian master. When his master saw that the Lord was with him and that the Lord gave him success in everything he did, Joseph found favor in his eyes and became

his attendant. Potiphar put him in charge of his household, and he entrusted to his care everything he owned. From the time he put him in charge of his household and of all that he owned, the Lord blessed the household of the Egyptian because of Joseph. The blessing of the Lord was on everything Potiphar had, both in the house and in the field. So Potiphar left everything he had in Joseph's care; with Joseph in charge, he did not concern himself with anything except the food he ate.

God had promised Abraham his offspring would be a blessing to the whole world (Genesis 12:2–3), and we see it happening through Joseph. Potiphar's household was blessed because Joseph "found favor." God was present and at work in Joseph, and God's favor was Joseph's asset. Potiphar left the management to Joseph and didn't worry. This was the first of many promotions Joseph received. He went from being a common slave to a chosen servant, from being a common prisoner to a chosen prison keeper, from common house arrest to chosen house manager, from common misfortune to uncommon favor. His life was a powerful foreshadowing of Paul's hymn about Jesus Christ.

Have this mind among yourselves, which is yours in Christ Jesus, who, though he was in the form of God, did not count equality with God a thing to be grasped, but emptied himself, taking the form of a servant, being born in the likeness of men. And being found in human form he humbled himself and became obedient unto death, even death on a cross. Therefore God has highly exalted him and bestowed on him the name which is above every name, that at the name of Jesus every knee should bow, in heaven and on earth and under the earth, and every tongue confess that Jesus Christ is Lord, to the glory of God the Father. (Philippians 2:5–11 RSV)

Never forget your asset: where God's people are faithful, God will be known. Through faithful Jews, God was known in Egypt. Many a Sodom has been spared and blessed because of faithful followers of God, and many nations have been blessed because of the witness of God's people. God is present and at work in the lives of the faithful; His presence is mentioned five times in these five verses. He does not abandon us or leave us alone. We may be separated from family and friends, but we're not separated from God. Remember Jesus' promise to His disciples when he sent them out just before He ascended to heaven.

> Jesus, undeterred, went right ahead and gave his charge: "God authorized and commanded me to commission you: Go out and train everyone you meet, far and near, in this way of life, marking them by baptism in the threefold name: Father, Son, and Holy Spirit. Then instruct them in the practice of all I have commanded you. I'll be with you as you do this, day after day after day, right up to the end of the age." (Matthew 28:18–20 MSG)

When you faithfully do the best you can with what you have and where you are, you can count on God being present and at work. That's a powerful asset.

One night, I was on call as a chaplain for the police department. Dispatch asked me to go to the scene of a triple homicide. A mother and her two daughters had been brutally murdered, and the prime suspect was the mother's son. My main task then was to wait for the husband, who was on his way home from work. He didn't know of the tragedy. I had a good hour or so to wonder what to say, how to offer him support or comfort, and even wonder if there was anything I could offer.

As it played out, between his conversation with an outstanding, compassionate detective and a precious family member who was allowed at the scene, I needed to say little. But I'll never forget that as we said our parting words under the blackness of the night, he embraced me and said, "Thank you." He never saw the tears in my eyes. The tears were for him but also in response to a gracious Lord whose promise was fulfilled again: "I'll be with you as you do this, day after day after day, right up to the end of the age." I was overwhelmed with the priceless thought that when we faithfully do the best we can with what we have where we are, we can count on God being present and at work.

There's a second asset: God's presence makes whatever we do for Him prosper. We give our best, and God does the rest. In 41:37–38, we read, "So Pharaoh asked them, 'Can we find anyone like this man, one in whom is the spirit of God?'" Isn't it wonderful? We work, we remain faithful, and God does the rest! We don't have to worry about the results. If we're faithful where we are, God will bring the blessing. Missionary J. Hudson Taylor said, "God's work done in God's way will never lack God's supply."[14] As Paul wrote in Galatians 6:9, "Let us not become weary in doing good, for at the proper time we will reap a harvest if we do not give up." And Peter wrote, "Humble yourselves, therefore, under God's mighty hand, that he may lift you up in due time. Cast all your anxiety on him for he cares for you … And the God of all grace … will himself restore you and make you strong, firm and steadfast" (1 Peter 5:6–7, 10).

Consider a nineteen-year-old woman who, after being hurt severely by officials, was roughly thrown into a dark dungeon. The floor was wet. There was no bed. The smell was putrid. Rats and vermin were everywhere. Yet she thanked the Lord she was worthy to suffer for Him. She had refused to denounce her Savior, and for that, she was alone, hurt, but weeping tears of joy as her cell became her house of peace. She prayed to her Savior not for escape but for wisdom and strength, asking that wherever He put her, she would be able to continue to preach His gospel.

The days passed, and as she sat quietly singing a hymn, the Lord gave her a message: *This is to be your ministry.* Unclear as to what this meant, she continued to pray that her ministry would be fulfilled. Her Savior spoke to her. She called for the guard. "Sir, this prison is so dirty. There is human waste everywhere. Let me go into the cells and clean up this filthy place. All you will have to do is give me some water and a brush."

She was soon on her hands and knees cleaning and preaching. She was looking into the faces of people unrecognizable as human beings. Through continuous poor treatment, they had lost all hope of ever seeing another human being who didn't come to hurt them. As they realized they could have eternal life, they fell on the dirty floor and repented of their sins, and soon, all the prisoners believed in Jesus Christ.

When the Communist officials found out about this, they were furious for having lost control over their prisoners. No matter what the officials did, the prisoners would only say, "We forgive you in the name of Jesus." So they told her to write a confession of her sins against the state. In answer to her unspoken prayer, words slowly came to her. She handed the confession to the guard to be delivered to the warden, who called her into his office. He was enraged by the antirevolutionary things she had written. He read her confession to a large group of people. It was the Lord's plan of salvation for all. Some were greatly moved by her written plan of salvation.

> Humble yourselves, therefore, under God's mighty hand, that he may lift you up in due time. Cast all your anxiety on him for he cares for you … And the God of all grace … will himself restore you and make you strong, firm and steadfast.[15]

When you are trapped in the pit, count your assets. Be faithful, and God will take care of the rest.

When you've made an attitude adjustment and counted your assets, you'll develop an advancement awareness of God's work. God's plan to lead Israel to the Promised Land continued through Joseph; His work was being carried forward. Joseph's life was spared even if through slavery for the purpose of the kingdom. When the time of great famine came, he was prepared in a position to save his family and people; it was part of God's plan. Where we see rejection, God sees progress. Where we see hurdles, God sees a leap forward. Where we see stumbling blocks, God sees stepping stones. His plan will not fail.

I still recall an illustration used by Jay Kesler years ago while he was head of Youth for Christ. He pointed to an automobile assembly line down which frames were moving and receiving tires from Detroit, mirrors from Holland, and other parts from all over. Those who made the tires and mirrors didn't see the final product; they just made what they were supposed to. Then, as the frame moved down the line everything was added at just the right time. And in the end, everything came together. He related this to God's plan— many people doing many seemingly unrelated things. God weaves them together at just the right time and way, and the finished product is what He designed. It's the same with the pitfalls of your life. God is advancing His work. Paul wrote, "And we know that in all things God works for the good of those who love him, who have been called according to his purpose" (Romans 8:28).

Whatever you've been through and whatever you're going through is part of God's preparation of you for the next phase of His plan. A dear, older man in one of my pastorates had been diagnosed with cancer but was vibrant with faith. An avid singer, he introduced his solo in a cantata by saying, "We need to accept this phase of God's plan before He can move us to the next one." His pitfall was a launching pad for greater testimony. Whatever your situation, God is preparing you for the next phase of His plan just as He prepared Joseph for future situations and responsibilities. Joseph would one day be confronted with the choice of retaliation against or forgiveness of his brothers; what he had experienced of God prepared him to make a godly choice. Joseph wasn't bound by his circumstances but by God.

As you sit at the bottom of your pit feeling trapped by the circumstances of life, maybe you're wondering about God—where He is and why He doesn't seem to be doing anything to help you. You're beginning to think He's ignoring you or has even forgotten you. No! God is preparing you for the next phase of His plan.

When you're feeling trapped, when your life is in the pit, let go of whatever you're clinging so tightly to and get a grip on faith. Be more concerned about what you bring to life than what life brings to you. Turn your pitfall into a launching pad. Bring your faith into your situation. Adjust your attitude, count your assets, and advance God's plan. Be faithful where you are; keep writing your story. Jesus said, "My sheep listen to my voice; I know them, and they follow me. I give them eternal life, and they shall never perish; no one can snatch them out of my hand" (John 10:27–28). Look up from your pit. See Jesus on the cross, His arms stretched out reaching for you. Take His hand and hang on for the ride. Ira Stanphill wrote, "Many things about tomorrow I don't seem to understand; But I know who holds tomorrow, And I know who holds my hand."[16]

For Your Reflection

I don't know about tomorrow, I just live from day to day;
I don't borrow from its sunshine, For its skies may turn to gray.
I don't worry o'er the future, For I know what Jesus said;
And today I'll walk beside Him, For He knows what is ahead.

Ev'ry step is getting brighter As the golden stairs I climb
Ev'ry burden's getting lighter Ev'ry cloud is silver-lined
There the sun is always shining There no tear will dim the eye
At the ending of the rainbow Where the mountains touch the sky

I don't know about tomorrow, It may bring me poverty;
But the one who feeds the sparrow, Is the one who stands by me.
And the path that is my portion, May be through the flame or flood;
But His presence goes before me, And I'm covered with His blood.

Many things about tomorrow I don't seem to understand;
But I know who holds tomorrow, And I know who holds my hand.[17]

CHAPTER 3

When the Going Gets Tough ... Temptation Becomes Testimony

Genesis 39:6–23

Joseph flees Potiphar's seduction (used with permission from iStock.com)

Temptation: the state of being allured, seduced.

A minister parked his car in a no-parking zone and attached the following message to his windshield: "I have circled this block ten times. I have an appointment to keep. Forgive our trespasses." When he returned to his car, he found this reply attached to his own note along with a ticket: "I've circled this block for ten years. If I don't give you a ticket, I lose my job. Lead us not into temptation."

It's easy to joke about temptation. Oscar Wilde was said to have written, "I can resist anything—except temptation." I once saw a T-shirt emblazoned with, "Lead me not into temptation—I can find it for myself." We all know temptation well; we face it daily. After Joseph rose from being a mere slave to head of Potiphar's household, the going got tough again; he faced severe temptation. As we study this time in his life, we discover that for every temptation, there's an escape that if followed will make times of temptation become times of testimony.

Think about the power of temptation. Joseph was at that point about twenty-seven; it had been about ten years since he had been betrayed by his brothers. He had developed into a fine young man not only in terms of maturity and leadership but physically as well. He was a hunk, a stud; his body was finely tuned, and his features were impeccable. He took his job seriously and performed his duties diligently. With Joseph in charge of his household, Potiphar, his master, didn't have a care in the world. Then one day, Potiphar's wife invited Joseph to bed with her, and she had more in mind than just napping; she invited him repeatedly. Joseph was experiencing temptation.

Temptation is the state of being allured, seduced; it's to be offered the opportunity to do something evil or unwise with a promise of pleasure or gain. Temptation occurs in all realms of our lives—mental, emotional, physical, and spiritual. I saw a movie about a woman who unknowingly married into the Mafia. At the end of the movie, as she is finally freed from her husband, he tries to explain his actions: "When the devil shows up with a boatload of promises, it's harder than ever to walk away."[18] This was Joseph's situation. While this chapter deals with temptation in all its forms, Scripture clearly and repeatedly shows sexual temptation to be a consistent stumbling block for the people of God.

- David withstood evil advances until he saw Bathsheba.
- Samson was filled with all the power of God until he gave in to the alluring voice of Delilah.

- Members of the Corinthian church were on fire for the Lord but had great difficulty letting go of their sexual immorality.
- Today, one of the most common temptations for a preacher or Christian leader is that of sexual immorality.

So this picture of Joseph is as real as today's headline. Let's come to grips with the characteristics of temptation. First, temptation is common to all; none of us escapes it. If you're alive, you'll be tempted. In its section on the Lord's Prayer, the Heidelberg Catechism asks why we should ever have to pray, "Lead us not into temptation." The answer is, "Since we are so weak that we cannot stand by ourselves for one moment, and besides, since our sworn enemies, the devil, the world, and our own sin, ceaselessly assail us."[19] Our human nature is weak and susceptible to attack.

Occasionally, people suggest to me that it must be wonderful to be a minister, and it is. But they go on to talk about ministers being able to spend so much time in the Word, walking so closely with the Lord, and apparently therefore being immune to life as a normal person. The implication is that ministers' lives are so much more spiritual that they're more protected from temptation. I face temptation daily. In fact, as a minister, I'm sometimes a priority target of the tempter. I'm constantly tempted to grab at the power available to me, which is significant. The drive to be successful often tempts me. The need to be popular is alluring. The temptation to be lazy is great, as is the temptation to never take a day off and become a workaholic. And the potential for sexual temptation is greater than you probably want to know. I'm no more immune to temptation than you are.

Thinking that certain people are more immune to temptation than others is tantamount to claiming Jesus was more immune to temptation than we are since He was the Son of God. Yet Hebrews 4:15 (GNT) reminds us, "Our High Priest is not one who cannot feel sympathy for our weaknesses. On the contrary, we have a High Priest who was tempted in every way that we are, but did not sin."

A second characteristic of temptation is that it often comes when least expected, like lightning. It didn't strike Joseph when he was in the pit or was the lowest of slaves but when he was exercising great leadership and experiencing great success. Likewise, Jesus was tempted after the exhilaration of His baptism. The higher the ladder, the greater the danger; the bigger the fires of success, the more the heat. It's like the ending to the old *Candid Camera* TV show when Allen Funt, the host, would say, "Sometime, someplace, when you least expect it ..." That's when temptation often strikes. That's why the Apostle Paul wrote "If you think you are standing firm, be careful that you don't fall" (1 Corinthians 10:12). *The Message* puts this verse in a clear light: "Don't be so naive and self-confident. You're not exempt. You could fall flat on your face as easily as anyone else. Forget about self-confidence; it's useless." Always be on guard.

Part of the reason we least expect it is that the tempter's attacks are often very subtle. Have you ever visited the *Spy Museum* in downtown Washington, DC? It's a phenomenal experience; it covers the history of spying throughout the world. To see all the ways and means by which spying has occurred is fascinating—and sobering. To learn of all the gadgets and deceitful implements used is eye-opening—and overwhelming. It's a vivid reminder of the subtlety with which Satan often tempts us. John Henry Jowett affirmed this subtlety.

> Evil enticements always come to us in borrowed attire. In the Boer War ammunition was carried out in piano cases, and military advices were transported in the skins of melons. And that is the way of the enemy of our souls. He makes us think we are receiving music when he is sending us explosives; he promises life, but his gift is laden with the hides of death. He offers us liberty, and he hides his chains in dazzling flowers. "Things are not what they seem."[20]

Third, temptation strikes where you're most susceptible. Each of us has a breaking point. We might not know what it is, but Satan does. Even Achilles had his breaking point. His mother dipped him in the river Styx, believing it had magical power to protect him. But then an arrow struck him where she had held his heel to dip him, and he died! Satan will bring us into contact with our breaking point; he will attack our Achilles heel every chance he gets. He'll lead the compulsive gambler to the casino, the addict to the dealer, and the alcoholic to the bar; he'll lead the person with lust to the places where sex runs freely; he'll put the person who craves power into situations where power must be had at any cost.

Some drug dealers once went to the captain of an oil tanker that regularly made trips from South America to Los Angeles. They offered him $10,000 to bring in a load of cocaine. He refused. They came back another day and offered $50,000. Again, he refused. They came one more time and offered $150,000. That time, he said he would think about it. He did—and called the FBI. They put together a sting operation and caught the drug runners. They seized the shipment of drugs, $340,000 worth, and a list of buyers in the LA area. After the arrest, one of the agents asked the captain, "Why did you wait until they offered you $150,000 before you called us?" He replied, "They were getting pretty close to my price, and I was scared."

You're contending not only against flesh and blood but against principalities, powers, the rulers of darkness, against the spiritual hosts of wickedness in the heavenly places (see Ephesians 6:10–12). Satan knows your breaking point and will attack it.

The fourth characteristic of temptation is that it arouses desires in us. If the world or Satan couldn't offer something we really wanted, they'd have no power over us. All Satan does is put the bait in front of us; we swallow it. Remember the words of James 1:14: "Each one is tempted when, by his own evil desire, he is dragged away and enticed. Then, after desire has conceived, it gives birth to sin." The tempter's bait simply arouses desires already in us.

Understand that desire is not necessarily bad. In itself, it's neutral. So Satan most often puts something on his hook that is good. Good desire can result in sinful actions. The desire to own and possess can lead to theft. The pleasure of eating can lead to gluttony. The desire to be loved, to be warmed by human touch, to fulfill the divine sexual drive can lead to adultery. The desire to succeed and gain a position of influence can lead to cheating. To be tempted is to be lured to fulfill good desires in a wrong way.

Perhaps that's why *The Message* puts James 1:14–15 this way: "The temptation to give in to evil comes from us and only us. We have no one to blame but the leering, seducing flare-up of our own lust. Lust gets pregnant, and has a baby: sin!" Is it any wonder that the apostle Paul so bluntly and accurately shared the human struggle this way?

> I realize that I don't have what it takes. I can will it, but I can't *do* it. I decide to do good, but I don't *really* do it; I decide not to do bad, but then I do it anyway. My decisions, such as they are, don't result in actions. Something has gone wrong deep within me and gets the better of me. (Romans 7:18–20 MSG)

Dietrich Bonhoeffer described it eloquently.

> In our members there is a slumbering inclination towards desire which is both sudden and fierce. With irresistible power desire seizes mastery over the flesh. All at once a secret, smouldering fire is kindled. The flesh burns and is in flames. It makes no difference whether it is sexual desire, or ambition, or vanity, or desire for revenge, or love of fame and power, or greed for money, or, finally that strange desire for the beauty of the world, of nature. Joy in God is in course of being extinguished in us and we seek all our joy in the creature. At this moment God is quite unreal to us, he loses all reality, and only desire for the creature is real; the only reality is the devil. Satan does not here fill us with hatred of God, but with forgetfulness of God ... The lust thus aroused envelops the mind and will of man in deepest darkness. The powers of clear discrimination and of decision are taken from us ... It is here that everything within me rises up against the Word of God.[21]

When you're tempted, be aware of and sensitive to your desires, needs, and drives and strengthen your resolve to stand firm. You can stand firm because as powerful as temptation is, we learn from Joseph and the rest of Scripture that while the way out might differ from situation to situation, there's an escape from temptation. Fortunately, God knows our breaking point also. Paul wrote,

> No temptation has seized you except what is common to man. And God is faithful; he will not let you be tempted beyond

what you can bear. But when you are tempted, he will also provide a way out so that you can endure it. (1 Corinthians 10:13)

The Bible offers several ways to get out of temptation. The first step is refusal: just say no. Look again at Joseph's situation.

Now Joseph was well-built and handsome, and after a while his master's wife took notice of Joseph and said, "Come to bed with me!" But he refused. "With me in charge," he told her, "my master does not concern himself with anything in the house; everything he owns he has entrusted to my care. No one is greater in this house than I am. My master has withheld nothing from me except you, because you are his wife. How then could I do such a wicked thing?" (Genesis 39:6–9)

Notice what the text says next: "And though she spoke to Joseph day after day, he refused to go to bed with her or even be with her." Joseph said no repeatedly; there's always a choice.

An old Indian legend reportedly told by Iron Eyes says it well.

Many years ago, Indian youths would go away in solitude to prepare for manhood. One such youth hiked into a beautiful valley, green with trees, bright with flowers. There he fasted. But on the third day, as he looked up at the surrounding mountains, he noticed one tall, rugged peak, capped with dazzling snow. "I will test myself on that mountain," he thought. He put on his buffalo hide shirt, threw his blanket over his shoulders, and set off to climb the peak. When he reached the top he stood on the rim of the world. He could see forever, and his heart swelled with pride. Then he heard a rustle at his feet, and looking down, he saw a snake. Before he could move, the snake spoke: "I am about to die. It is too cold for me up here and I am freezing. There is no food and I am starving. Put me under your shirt and take me down into the valley." "No" said the youth. "I am forewarned. I know your kind. You are a rattlesnake. If I pick you up, you will bite, and your bite will kill me."

"Not so," said the snake. "I will treat you differently. If you do this for me, you will be special. I will not harm you." The youth resisted awhile, but this was a very persuasive snake with beautiful markings. At last the youth tucked it under his shirt and carried it down to the valley. There he laid it gently on the grass, when suddenly the snake coiled, rattled, and leapt, biting him on the leg. "But you promised," cried the youth. "You knew what I was when you picked me up," said the snake as it slithered away. [22]

"You knew what I was when you picked me up"; there is always a choice. Refuse. God will not give you more than you can bear and will provide a way out.

The second step in the process of escape is to do the right thing. Notice how Joseph, in refusing Potiphar's wife, grounded his choice to say no: "How then can I do such a wicked thing and sin against God?" Joseph chose to remember his duty to God; he turned temptation into testimony. Clarence Macartney wrote of this scene.

This was no ordinary temptation. Joseph was not a stone, a mummy, but a red-blooded young man in his late twenties. It was not one temptation on one day, but a repeated temptation … An old story tells how when Joseph began to talk about God to the temptress, she flung her skirt over the bust of the god that stood in the chamber and said, "Now, God will not see." But Joseph answered, "My God sees!"[23]

We have a duty to God; His standards are those of right and wrong. To do wrong is to cut ourselves off from God; sin offends Him, defies His authority, abuses His goodness, and insults His intelligence. Make decisions based on principle, not profit. Through the prophet Micah, God said, "He has showed you, O man, what is good; and what does the LORD require of you but to do justice, and to love kindness, and to walk humbly with your God?" (Micah 6:8 RSV). Do the right no matter what. Turn your temptation into testimony.

Remember Shadrach, Meshach, and Abednego? The king demanded they bow and worship him or be thrown into the fiery furnace. Their response?

> Your threat means nothing to us. If you throw us in the fire, the God we serve can rescue us from your roaring furnace and anything else you might cook up, O king. But even if he doesn't, it wouldn't make a bit of difference, O king. We still wouldn't serve your gods or worship the gold statue you set up. (Daniel 3:16–18 MSG)

That's choosing the right. They turned their temptation into testimony.

Peter and John were called before the Sanhedrin, whose members were disturbed by their preaching. They ordered the apostles to stop preaching and teaching in the name of Jesus. "But Peter and John replied, 'Which is right in God's eyes: to listen to you, or to him? You be the judges! As for us, we cannot help speaking about what we have seen and heard.'" (Acts 4:19–20). That's choosing the right. They turned their temptation into a testimony.

After fasting forty days and nights in the desert, Jesus was tempted in three ways by the tempter. Here are Jesus' responses.

> It is written: "Man shall not live on bread alone, but on every word that comes from the mouth of God" … It is also written: "Do not put the Lord your God to the test … Away from me, Satan!" For it is written: "Worship the Lord your God, and serve him only." (Matthew 4:4, 7, 10–11)

That's choosing the right and the result was powerful: "Then the devil left him, and angels came and attended him." The power and wisdom of choosing the right is that it keeps you from giving in when you're tempted and turns your temptation into testimony.

The third step of escape is running away from the fire. Verse 12 says Potiphar's wife grabbed Joseph's cloak but Joseph "left his cloak in her hand and ran out of the house." God promises no help if you stick around.

Someone once said, "Watch out for temptation—the more you see of it the better it looks."[24] With flammable desires in your life, get away from the flame. You cannot take explosives into flames without producing an explosion. Jesus said that if your right hand offends, you are to cut it off—meaning get it out of the way. As Matthew Henry said, "It is better to lose a good coat than a good conscience." What would have happened to history if David had run rather than stood on the balcony staring at Bathsheba?

Jack Handey, known for his odd sense of humor frequently expressed in an old *Saturday Night Live* segment titled "Deep Thoughts," wrote an equally odd book entitled *Fuzzy Memories*. In it, he related the story of a bully who demanded his lunch money every day when he was a child. Because Handey was smaller than the bully, he simply gave the bully his money. "Then I decided to fight back," Handey wrote. "I started taking karate lessons, but the instructor wanted $5 a lesson. That was a lot of money. I found that it was cheaper to pay the bully, so I gave up karate."[25] Unfortunately, many people have the same attitude about Satan and the temptations that come their way: it's easier to pay the bully than to learn how to fight him. Joseph knew better; he ran no matter what the cost.

Some years ago, the Israeli government's tourist office advertised trips to Israel with a full-page ad that showed a smiling man sitting in a relaxed position with his legs crossed and a teacup in his hand, floating on the Dead Sea. The ad read, "Cups and saucers float on it … And so do you … You can float clear to Sodom if you like." If we stick around temptation, we float closer to Sodom. I wonder if the tourist office was aware of what happened when Abram gave Lot the opportunity to choose his fields. Lot chose the plush fields near the Jordan River. "Abram dwelt in the land of Canaan, while Lot dwelt among the cities of the valley and moved his tent as far as Sodom. Now the men of Sodom were wicked, great sinners against the LORD." (Genesis 13:12–13 RSV). And he all but floated into Sodom.

Is it any wonder that Scripture repeatedly orders us to flee temptation? "Run from anything that stimulates youthful lusts. Instead, pursue righteous living, faithfulness, love, and peace. Enjoy the companionship of those who call on the Lord with pure hearts" (2 Timothy 2:22 NLT). "Run from sexual sin! No other sin so clearly affects the body as this one does. For sexual immorality is a sin against your own body" (1 Corinthians 6:18 NLT). "Therefore, my dear friends, flee from idolatry" (1 Corinthians 10:14).

When faced with temptation, don't stand there and debate the issue. Run! Don't weigh the merits of the situation. Run! Don't try to convince someone else you can hold on, decide to see how strong you are by sticking around, or fool yourself by saying, "It never hurts just to look." Run, and don't leave a forwarding address.

For every temptation, there is a way of escape. What allures you, seduces you, pulls you, tugs at you in such a way that it leads you to the precipice of sin? Run!

There is a fourth step of escape—having a right relationship. Recall whose you are. George Sweeting wrote, "Every temptation is an opportunity for us to draw near to God."[26] A good way of drawing near is to remind yourself, "I am not my own, but belong body and soul, in life and in death to my faithful Savior Jesus Christ. He has fully paid for all my sins with his precious blood, and has also set me free from the tyranny of the devil."[27] Those marvelous words can serve as a powerful reminder to guard your heart. As Proverbs 4:23 states, "Above all else, guard your heart, for everything you do flows from it."

Remember the breech is made in the dam before the floodwaters rise. Listening to the tempter always precedes the fall. What matters is not the outside forces but the inside fortresses. If you want to get rid of darkness, let in light. If you want to get rid of weeds, plant grass. If you want to keep evil out of your heart, be sure the Lord Jesus Christ is in it. Your heart must be so filled with Christ that when the tempter comes, he will find the heart so preoccupied that he will leave for lack of room.

Martin Luther was often very graphic in his description of the activities of the devil. Asked one time how he overcame the devil, he replied,

> Well, when he comes knocking upon the door of my heart, and asks "Who lives here?" the dear Lord Jesus goes to the door and says, "Martin Luther used to live here but he has moved out. Now I live here." The Devil seeing the nail-prints in the hands, and the pierced sides, takes flight immediately.[28]

Turning your temptations into testimonies is possible because once you've given Jesus control of your life, He will fill you with the Holy Spirit.

As John wrote (1 John 4:4), "…the one who is in you is greater than the one who is in the world." Paul wrote,

> Live by the Spirit, and you will not gratify the desires of the sinful nature. (Galatians 5:16)

> So you also should consider yourselves to be dead to the power of sin and alive to God through Christ Jesus. Do not let sin control the way you live; do not give in to sinful desires. Do not let any part of your body become an instrument of evil to serve sin. Instead, give yourselves completely to God, for you were dead, but now you have new life. So use your whole body as an instrument to do what is right for the glory of God. Sin is no longer your master, for you no longer live under the requirements of the law. Instead, you live under the freedom of God's grace. (Romans. 6:11–14 NLT)

> Therefore put on the full armor of God, so that when the day of evil comes, you may be able to stand your ground, and after you have done everything, to stand. (Ephesians 6:13)

Perhaps you're thinking that saying no is too hard, that you don't have the energy to run, that you've fallen out of touch with the Spirit. Maybe the guilt of your giving in to temptation is weighing heavily on you. Listen to Solomon's wisdom: "For though the righteous fall seven times, they rise again" (Proverbs 24:16). Jesus died and rose so you could keep rising. Through His grace, He has forgiven you; as often as you have fallen, He has forgiven you. He sees a testimony in your temptation and wants nothing more than for it to become your story.

Remember whose you are. Let Jesus rule your heart and mind. Leave no vacancy there. Learn the lesson of the obedient dog. When a bit of meat is placed on the floor near an obedient dog and the master says "No," the dog will usually takes its eyes off the meat because the temptation is too great. Instead, it will fix its eyes on its master's face.

Only you know what you're wrestling with. If temptation is getting the better of you, turn your eyes to Jesus and look full in His wonderful face; open up and clean out your heart to let Jesus in. If you aren't facing any temptation, be grateful but take heed lest you fall. You too must turn your eyes to Jesus; the things of earth will grow dim in the light of His glory and grace. Refuse the devil's offerings. Turn to Jesus and turn your temptation into your testimony. Heed the invitation in Hebrews 4:15–16 (GNT).

> Our High Priest is not one who cannot feel sympathy for our weaknesses. On the contrary, we have a High Priest who was tempted in every way that we are, but did not sin. Let us have confidence, then, and approach God's throne, where there is grace. There we will receive mercy and find grace to help us just when we need it.

For Your Reflection

O soul, are you weary and troubled?
No light in the darkness you see?
There's a light for a look at the Savior,
And life more abundant and free!

Through death into life everlasting
He passed, and we follow Him there;
Over us sin no more hath dominion—
For more than conquerors we are!

His Word shall not fail you—He promised;
Believe Him, and all will be well:
Then go to a world that is dying,
His perfect salvation to tell!

Turn your eyes upon Jesus,
Look full in His wonderful face,
And the things of earth will grow strangely dim,
In the light of His glory and grace.[29]

CHAPTER 4

When the Going Gets Tough ...
Rejections Become Opportunities

Genesis 40:1–23

Joseph interprets dreams

Rejection: to refuse to accept a person; rebuff; to throw away or discard as useless or unsatisfactory; to cast out, cast off, or eject.

While in junior high, I was asked to serve on a committee to revamp the student government because I'd been the "mayor" of our elementary school government. The intent was to consider changing from the traditional student-council style to a city-commission form.

After several meetings, we decided we needed a proposal, and I said I'd write one up. After a number of hours and some late nights, I'd put together something for the next meeting. At the meeting, the faculty advisor said that she didn't think we needed any change, that the current form was working well, and she thanked us for our work. That was it! Not even any consideration of the proposal. I felt rejected. I wondered if being nice really paid.

A church reaches out to a family through counseling, financial assistance, home repairs, and the like. Untold hours are spent meeting their needs. Then one day, a staff member confronts a member of the family concerning some aspect of his or her life, and the family bolts from the church, bad-mouths the congregation, and spreads malicious and untrue stories about it. The congregation and staff feel rejected and wonder if being nice really pays.

I have an idea that you too have felt rejected and wondered if being nice really paid. That's why we can identify with Joseph. There's probably not a nicer person in Scripture except for Jesus. Yet on more than one occasion when Joseph did something nice, misfortune or tragedy overtook him; his niceness led to his rejection.

Joseph had righteously fled from the sexual advances of Potiphar's wife only to be double-crossed by her and thrown into prison. Rejection. Had being nice paid? As nice a person as Joseph was, he had spent about a third of his life in captivity. Rejection. Did being nice pay?

Think about early Christendom. In the *Letter to Diognetus*, which dates to the second century AD, the writer described a strange people.

> Christians are not differentiated from other people by country, language, or customs; you see, they do not live in cities of their own, or speak some strange dialect … They live in both Greek and foreign cities, wherever chance has put them. They follow local customs in clothing, food, and other aspects of life. But at the same time, they demonstrate to us an unusual form of their own citizenship.

They live in their own native lands, but as aliens ... Every foreign country is to them as their native country, and every native land as a foreign country.

They marry and have children just like everyone else, but they do not kill unwanted babies. They offer a shared table, but not a shared bed. They are passing their days on earth, but are citizens of heaven. They obey the appointed laws and go beyond the laws in their own lives.

They love everyone, but they are persecuted by all. They are put to death and gain life. They are poor and yet make many rich. They are dishonored and yet gain glory through dishonor. Their names are blackened and yet they are cleared. They are mocked and bless in return. They are treated outrageously and behave respectfully to others.

When they do good, they are punished as evildoers; when punished, they rejoice as if being given new life. They are attacked by Jews as aliens and are persecuted by Greeks; yet those who hate them cannot give any reason for their hostility.[30]

Rejection. Did being nice pay?

Genesis 40 demonstrates that times of rejection are really moments of opportunity. Through each rejection, Joseph had an opportunity to learn, serve, and grow. God was training Joseph through all his rejections for leadership.

Verses 1–3 again raise the issue of God's sovereignty. They underscore first of all God's providence. We meet here the chief cupbearer and the chief cook. The cupbearer had to sample all drinks before Pharaoh drank them; he eventually became a bodyguard responsible for Pharaoh's safety. He and the cook were the ruler's right-hand people. Somehow, they angered Pharaoh and were put into prison; they were eventually assigned to Joseph. Joseph of course was in prison because he had rejected the sexual advances of Potiphar's wife only to be rejected in turn by her and Potiphar.

The scene serves as a reminder that there are no chance encounters for God's people. God is involved in the events of your life. In answer to the question, "What do you understand by the providence of God?" the Heidelberg Catechism proclaims,

> The almighty and ever-present power of God whereby he still upholds, as it were by his own hand, heaven and earth together with all creatures, and rules in such a way that leaves and grass, rain and drought, fruitful and unfruitful years, food and drink, health and sickness, riches and poverty, and everything else, come to us not by chance but by his fatherly hand. [31]

Think about Joseph. Were his dreams of leadership just chance happenings? Was it mere chance the Ishmaelites came by after his brothers had thrown him into a pit to die? Was it mere coincidence that Potiphar purchased him as a slave? Was it chance that Joseph was in prison when the cupbearer and the cook arrived? Was it chance that Joseph could interpret their dreams?

It's amazing to see how Joseph's experience at so many critical points touched others for a grand purpose. God finds ways often hidden to us to move us along His plan for us. When you read a good novel or mystery, you know there are no chance occurrences or happenings; you know every event has a significance. It is no less with God's authorship of your life. There are no chance encounters.

Late one evening, a professor sat at his desk working on the next day's lectures. He shuffled through the papers and mail placed there by his housekeeper. He began to throw them in the wastebasket when one magazine—not even addressed to him but delivered to his office by mistake— caught his attention. It fell open to an article entitled "The Needs of the Congo Mission." He began reading and was soon consumed by the words.

> The need is great here. We have no one to work in the northern province of Gabon in the central Congo. And it is my prayer as I write this article that God will lay His hand on one—one on whom, already, the Master's eyes have been cast - that he or she shall be called to this place to help us. [32]

The professor closed the magazine and wrote in his diary, "My search is over." At that moment, Albert Schweitzer committed himself to ministry in the Congo. Was that magazine mistakenly delivered by chance or intentionally delivered by God?

When Victor Frankl was first taken to a concentration camp, he lost the manuscript written in shorthand for the book eventually published as *The Doctor and the Soul*. However, in the pocket of his assigned prison clothes he found a copy of one page of a main Jewish prayer, Shema Yisrael. Believing with all his being that a person's life is determined not by what life brings but by the response he or she makes, he knew it was more than just coincidence or chance; it was a challenge to live out his faith where he was. Were those clothes mistakenly given him by chance or intentionally by God?

In 1968, I called the pastor in charge of hiring for our denominations' summer youth camp in Michigan, my home state. I asked if there were any openings for summer staff. He informed me that the camp was full but that there were openings at a new camp; he asked if I'd be interested in working there. I was, and I did. It was there that I met Barb, a nurse, who one year later became my precious wife. Was that one camp filled by chance or by the arrangement of God?

God's providence is the thread on which the events of your life are strung. Never forget—in fact, burn into your mind—that there are no chance encounters for God's people. Every situation in life, especially your rejections, are potential opportunities for furthering God's plan. The only issue is whether you will treat them as such.

God's sovereignty manifests itself in His providence and presence.

> But while Joseph was there in prison, the Lord was with him; he showed him kindness and granted him favor in the eyes of the prison warden. So the warden put Joseph in charge of all those held in the prison ... The warden paid no attention to anything under Joseph's care, because the Lord was with Joseph and gave him success in whatever he did. (Genesis 39:21)

God didn't just send Joseph to prison; He went with him! In the midst of his rejection, in the confines of his imprisonment, Joseph wasn't alone, and neither are you.

Simply because he was a member of the Confessing Church, Christian Reger was imprisoned in Dachau by the Nazis from 1941 to 1945. Talk about rejection—the organist of his church had turned him in! Philip Yancey wrote about Christian in his book *Where Is God When It Hurts?*

> Christian Reger will tell the horror stories if you ask. But he will never stop there. He goes on to share his faith—how at Dachau, he was visited by a God who loves. "Nietzsche said a man can undergo torture if he knows the why of his life," Reger told me. "But I, here at Dachau, learned something far greater. I learned the Who of my life. He was enough to sustain me then, and is enough to sustain me still."[33]

He was never alone. You are never alone. God is with you.

There's a story about a lighthouse that was built on the rocky coast of a remote island in the Pacific. The people there had never seen a lighthouse before. They had watched its construction with great interest and looked forward to its completion. When the big day came, they saw the light and heard the bells and horn during a heavy fog. After several hours, they disbanded in disgust. A project engineer proudly asked one of the natives what he thought. With a snort, he replied, "The light shines, the bell rings, the horn blows, but the fog keeps on just the same."

Have you ever missed the presence of God because you were too busy looking at the fog rather than the light? Can you say, "Even though I walk through the darkest valley I will fear no evil, for you are with me" (Psalm 23:4)? Do you believe Jesus' promise, "Lo, I am with you always"?

In the midst of your rejections, when you feel being nice doesn't pay, remember that God's sovereignty is at work. Everything comes to you not by chance but by His fatherly hand. Through His providence and presence, He will grant you progress and success. Your rejections can become opportunities.

But God's sovereignty by itself is not all there is; God invites our partnership in His plan. Joseph turned his rejection into an opportunity by responding to God's involvement in his life; he became a partner with God. Evident in the rest of this chapter are at least three qualities of his life that linked him to God's plan.

First, notice Joseph's character. He understood he was a coworker with God and always acted on that principle. He was the best slave, the best attendant of a ruler, a model prisoner, and the best prison official he could be. He didn't ask himself, *Why is this happening to me? After everything I've done for God, how does He dare let this happen to me?* He simply went about his daily tasks. Joseph didn't compromise to get promotions; he got promotions because he didn't compromise. Reputation is what others make of you; character is what you make of yourself. Reputation is what represents you; character is what shapes you. Reputation is what precedes you; character is what follows you. Reputation is how others view you; character is how God views you. Reputation is what is spoken in eulogies; character is what Jesus speaks to the Father when He presents you in glory.

In every rejection, you can choose bitterness or betterment, wondering or work, inaction or initiative. Yes, there will be frustrations, hurt, maybe even anger, but take them to the highest court. Let God take care of the wrongs and injustices done to you.

> Humble yourselves, therefore, under God's mighty hand, that he may lift you up in due time. Cast all your anxiety on him, because he cares for you. (1 Peter 5:7)

> Commit everything you do to the LORD. Trust him, and he will help you. He will make your innocence radiate like the dawn, and the justice of your cause will shine like the noonday sun. Be still in the presence of the LORD, and wait patiently for him to act. (Psalm 37:5–7 NLT)

God knows something about rejection. Jesus was unjustly accused, even illegally crucified, but He didn't retaliate, make threats, or claim his rights. And He was justified! He turned His rejections into opportunities, and so can you.

Hold on in every situation. Pursue your dreams. Like Joseph, be overwhelmed with God, not your circumstances. Take advantage of the opportunities God furnishes at critical times in your life, maintain your character, and see everything as an appointment from God. Seek to advance His cause and yours. You could fail in life not so much for lack of opportunities but for lack of character to maximize them.

A piece of solid metal opens into a tube when the heat reaches a precise temperature. If it gets too hot, it will burst; if it gets too cool, it will not open up but remain solid. The point at which the temperature is just right is called the molten moment, when perfecting occurs. Your situation might be a molten moment in which perfecting is about to occur. Let God set the temperature of your circumstances; don't fight the heat. Keep close to the flame of God. Live by His principles, and even if you're in prison, you can find a way to stand firm. Be a partner with God through your character; turn your rejections into opportunities.

Second, Joseph entered into partnership with God through his humility. Woodrow Wilson said, "If you will think about what you ought to do for other people, your character will take care of itself." In verses 4–8, Joseph noticed that the cupbearer and cook were sad, so he asked about that. When they mentioned their dreams, He testified that God could interpret them. Joseph knew that trials were doorways of opportunity to serve others. So did Paul, who wrote that God comforts us in our troubles so we can comfort others in trouble (2 Corinthians 1:3–4). People tuned into serving God consider the thoughts and feelings of others before their own. They see their rejections as opportunities.

Dietrich Bonhoeffer, a German minister born in 1906, became a respected scholar and theologian at a young age. He had great foresight, and he knew the Nazi party was an evil plague for Germany and the world. He became a powerful voice of German resistance. Bonhoeffer had visited the United States and was eventually offered a comfortable teaching position at one of America's distinguished seminaries. But he declined the offer; he returned to Germany and ministered to his people though he knew he was a marked man. Bonhoeffer knew what it meant to lower himself to the status of a servant. He was arrested by the Nazis in 1943, and on April 8, 1945, after conducting Sunday morning worship, he was hanged. As he was being led away, he remarked to an English officer who was also a prisoner of war, "This is the end, but for me the beginning of life." [34]

In God's economy, the way up is always down; it's the road of service. Scripture tells us that Jesus left the glories of heaven to become a servant (Philippians 2:5–11). He endured temptation so He could help those who were tempted; He suffered so He could help those who suffered; He died to help others live. He lived out what He preached: "The greatest among you will be your servant. For those who exalt themselves will be humbled, and those who humble themselves will be exalted" (Matthew 23:11–12).

Speaking of exaltation, notice that in offering to interpret the men's dreams, Joseph was really taking steps to fulfill his own. He soon ascended to a position of power and authority. When you are rejected, when nice doesn't pay, humble yourself. Use the trial and rejection as an opportunity to serve.

Joseph's third link to partnership with God was his contentment. Verse 23 tells us that after the cupbearer was released, he forgot his promise to remember Joseph. Joseph remained in prison, but he never quit expecting God to work. Most of us hate to wait; we're used to instant everything. But to cooperate with God, we need to be patient. Yes, it's tough when we've been rejected after being nice, and it happens all too frequently. The Rev. William Taylor succinctly wrote, "People too often write the record of grudges in marble and of favors in water."[35] That's true. Being nice doesn't always pay. Rejection happens. So contentedly wait, work, and serve.

This note of thanks paints the picture with masterful strokes:

> I want to thank you for what you have already done. I am not going to wait until I see the results or receive rewards, I am thanking you right now. I am not going to wait until I feel better or things look better, I am thanking you right now. I am not going to wait until people say they are sorry or until they stop talking about me. I am thanking you right now. I am not going to wait until the pain in my body disappears. I am thanking you right now. I am not going to wait until my financial situation improves. I am thanking you right now. I am not going to wait until the children are asleep and the house is quiet. I am thanking you right now. I am not going to wait until I get promoted at work or until I get the job. I am thanking you right now. I am not going to wait until I understand every experience in my life that has caused me pain or grief. I am thanking you right now. I am not going to wait

until the journey gets easier or the challenges are removed. I am thanking you right now. I am thanking you because I am alive. I am thanking you because I made it through the day's difficulties. I am thanking you because I have walked around the obstacles. I am thanking you because I have the ability and the opportunity to do more and do better. I am thanking you because you have not given up on me. God is just so good, and he's good all the time.[36]

Be content. Turn your rejections into opportunities. God's providence and presence are with you. Partner with God through your character, humility, and contentment. It's the best you can do when being nice ends in rejection.

So once again, we leave Joseph in what appears to be an unfair situation—still imprisoned, his favor and service forgotten. But we know that's not all there is. God was developing trust in Joseph; He was preparing him for leadership, and He wants to do the same for you. Jesus Christ is the same yesterday, today, and forever. He will not forget you, He will honor you.

> Come, you who are blessed by my Father; take your inheritance, the kingdom prepared for you since the creation of the world ... whatever you did for one of the least of these brothers and sisters of mine, you did for me. (Matthew 25:34, 40)

What you do in His name is written indelibly across His heart. The world may reject you, the world might forget you, you might have to endure a prison for a while, but just participate with God a little longer. Turn your rejections into opportunities and He will honor you.

I invite you to commit your rejections and your life to Jesus Christ, for in Him, all things hold together (Colossians 1:17). When being nice doesn't pay but ends in rejection, He will be the anchor of your soul.

For Your Reflection

Day by day, and with each passing moment,
Strength I find, to meet my trials here;
Trusting in my Father's wise bestowment,
I've no cause for worry or for fear.

He whose heart is kind beyond all measure
Gives unto each day what He deems best—
Lovingly, it's part of pain and pleasure,
Mingling toil with peace and rest.

Every day, the Lord Himself is near me
With a special mercy for each hour;
All my cares He fain would bear, and cheer me,
He whose name is Counselor and Power;
The protection of His child and treasure
Is a charge that on Himself He laid;
As thy days, thy strength shall be in measure,
This the pledge to me He made.

Help me then, in every tribulation
So to trust Thy promises, O Lord,
That I lose not faith's sweet consolation
Offered me within Thy holy Word.
Help me, Lord, when toil and trouble meeting,
E'er to take, as from a father's hand,
One by one, the days, the moments fleeting,
Till I reach the promised land.[37]

CHAPTER 5

When the Going Gets Tough ...
Prisons Become Promotions

Genesis 42:1–46

Joseph interpreting Pharaoh's dreams

Prisoner: one who is deprived of liberty or kept in restraint.

Paul Glock was imprisoned for his Anabaptist beliefs. His warden, Klaus von Grafeneck, had witnessed the martyrdom of a fellow Anabaptist twenty-five years earlier and was overcome when the martyr prayed for him just before he was executed. The warden allowed Paul to fetch wood, repair shoes, do odd jobs, and run errands on the condition he would not escape and would stay out of sight when strangers approached so his limited freedom wouldn't be discovered. Since his wife and child were dead, Paul had nothing to lose. So every day, Paul had a choice to make: escape or keep his word. If he escaped, Klaus would be in tremendous legal trouble and future imprisoned Anabaptists would be much more closely watched. Paul chose to keep his word.[38]

Prison is a tough place to be. Every time I've led worship in prison or visited prisoners there, I've left thinking, *I never want to live here. Why do people do things that send them here?* Perhaps that's why I'm always intrigued by stories and testimonies of those who have been imprisoned, especially unjustly, but make their cells sanctuaries. Perhaps you've visited a prison, but odds are you never called one home.

But the odds also are that at some time in your life, you've felt locked in, restrained against your will, not free to do or go where you want. That's a type of imprisonment. I'm not downplaying the dreadful, dreary, depressing life of prisoners, but we have all felt imprisoned emotionally, physically, or spiritually in other ways and felt depressed and devastated.

My senior year in high school was such a period for me. My high school was renowned for its choir, and I was an active member and leader of it. I was in the Honors Quartet and the State Honors Choir. By the time of my senior year, I had only two unfulfilled goals—to have a leading role on stage in our musical and to solo in our variety show. I also played cello in the orchestra. If I didn't get a lead role, I'd need to play in the orchestra, which is what I'd done previous years. Everyone thought I was a shoe-in for a solo and lead part my senior year, but long story short, it didn't happen. I sat in the orchestra pit devastated.

Things got more depressing when I went to college. I didn't qualify for a vocal music scholarship; I wasn't deemed good enough. Then I got my first semester grade in voice class—a C. That put my academic scholarship in jeopardy. I talked to my vocal teacher, who said that I had done all the work and had improved but that she graded on how close her students were to their potential. The good news was that she saw great potential in me. The bad news was that I was a long way from it. By that time, I truly felt restrained, limited, held back against my will, and emotionally and spiritually imprisoned. If only I had known then what I know now—that during such times, God is thoroughly preparing us for a greater position.

Our lives are constantly advancing toward the completion of God's plan for us. We're always getting ready for promotion. It's just that the imprisonments along the way tend to blur our perception of this great reality. If only I had learned from the attitudes and actions Joseph had demonstrated during his imprisonment. In this chapter, we'll discover the attitudes with which we are to live as we get ready for our next promotion.

The first attitude to transfer from Joseph is to release your control. You've already learned from Joseph that what appears to be bad times can be periods of significant growth and development. So engage in those activities and develop those attitudes that promote and facilitate growth. Whenever life appears bad and unfair or is simply in a lull, choose to believe God is at work developing you. It's the first step in releasing control.

A frequent phrase in the account of Joseph's life is, "the Lord was with Joseph." God was at work in, around, and through Joseph. God was working His plan for developing and promoting Joseph. If the cupbearer had remembered Joseph, Pharaoh would most likely either have moved Joseph to another location to still be a slave or at best released him so he could go home to Canaan. So God caused the cupbearer to forget until it was time to bring Joseph out of prison. While Joseph didn't know all these particulars, he did believe because of his dreams that God was at work developing him, so he remained faithful and willingly responded to Pharaoh's request for help. He let God take over.

Just what does it mean to let God take over? Vance Havner painted a great picture of that.

> Suppose I try to run a store. I know nothing about it, I get the books mixed up, I do not know how to buy or sell, things are in a dreadful mess. I turn the whole business over to another to own and manage and I become only a clerk in the same store I used to run. Mind you, I am as busy as ever but I have changed my responsibility. The care, the upkeep, the management, all that now is the owner's concern; my part is just to be a faithful clerk. "This Christ life is simply turning the little shop of life,

so woefully perplexing, over to another. Christ becomes owner, manager, overseer; his is the responsibility, the upkeep. Your part is to be a faithful clerk, steward of the grace of God. And one day, if you have been faithful over a few things, he will give you a heavenly shop in the city of the King!"[39]

That's letting God take over. Where and when have you let God take over in your life? Is there some imprisonment situation in your life you should submit to Him? Is your resistance holding back your promotion?

Since Joseph believed that God was faithfully at work developing him, he concentrated on being faithful to God. That brings into view the second step in releasing control: practice patient perseverance. Look at verse 1: "When two full years had passed, Pharaoh had a dream." For two years, Joseph experienced no reward for his kindness to the cupbearer and chief cook. At least on the surface, not much was happening, so Joseph waited for two years. We see repeatedly in the Bible that waiting was not unusual for God's people. Abraham waited until old age for the birth of Isaac. Moses waited until he was 80 to assume the mantle of leadership and lead Israel to freedom. Noah waited 120 years for rain. Yet all three grew to learn that God was at work developing them. Perseverance involves patient waiting.

The Reformed faith, which after the Bible has been the core of my theological training and study, strongly emphasizes this belief in patiently waiting as God does His sovereign work. This faith is summarized in several historical documents, one of which is entitled the Belgic Confession. Listen to what it says in article 13 (underlining mine):

We believe that this good God after he had created all things did not forsake them or give them up to chance or fortune, but that he so directs and governs them according to his holy will that nothing happens in this world outside his orderly arrangement, yet without being the author of sin or responsible for the sin that happens. For this might and goodness are so great and incomprehensible that he orders and executes his work well and righteously also when the devils and the godless act unrighteously. And as to what he does surpassing human understanding we will not curiously investigate beyond our capacity; but we will adore with all humility and reverence the righteous judgments of God that are hidden from us; <u>keeping ourselves content that we are pupils of Christ to learn only those things he shows us in his Word without transgressing these limits</u>.

Reflect for a moment on some of the testimonies of Scripture about patient waiting.

> I remain confident of this: I will see the goodness of the Lord in the land of the living. Wait for the Lord; be strong and take heart and wait for the Lord. (Psalm 27:13–14)

> I wait for the Lord, my whole being waits, and in his word I put my hope. I wait for the Lord more than watchmen wait for the morning, more than watchmen wait for the morning. (Psalm 130:5–6)

> Yet the Lord longs to be gracious to you; therefore he will rise up to show you compassion. For the Lord is a God of justice. Blessed are all who wait for him! (Isaiah 30:18)

> For the grace of God has appeared that offers salvation to all people. It teaches us to say "No" to ungodliness and worldly passions, and to live self-controlled, upright and godly lives in this present age, while we wait for the blessed hope—the appearing of the glory of our great God and Savior, Jesus Christ, who gave himself for us to redeem us from all wickedness and to purify for himself a people that are his very own, eager to do what is good. (Titus 2:11–14)

> So Christ, having been offered once to bear the sins of many, will appear a second time, not to deal with sin but to save those who are eagerly waiting for him. (Hebrews 9:28 RSV)

Releasing control by letting God take over through patiently waiting—it's the attitude that plants within our hearts the peace of God that passes all understanding. (Philippians 4:7)

There's a fable about a man sleeping in his cabin when suddenly his room filled with light and the Savior appeared. The Lord told the man that He had work for him to do and pointed to the large rock in front of his cabin. The Lord explained that the man was to push against the rock with all his might. This the man did day after day. For many years, he toiled from sunup to sundown, his shoulders set squarely against the cold, massive surface of the unmoving rock, pushing with all his might. Each night, he returned to his cabin sore and worn out, feeling his whole day had been spent in vain.

Seeing that the man was showing signs of discouragement, the adversary decided to enter the picture by placing thoughts in the man's weary mind: *You've been pushing that rock for a long time but it hasn't budged. Why kill yourself? You'll never move it.*

The man began to believe the task was impossible and that he was a failure. Eventually, the man became disheartened and thought, *Why kill myself over this? I'll just put in my time. Giving just the minimum effort will be good enough.*

And that is what he planned to do until one day he decided to make it a matter of prayer. "Lord," he prayed, "I have labored long and hard in your service, putting all my strength to do what you asked. Yet after all this time, I haven't budged that rock by half a millimeter. What's wrong? Why am I failing?"

The Lord responded compassionately, "My friend, when I asked you to serve me and you accepted, I told you that your task was to push against the rock with all your strength, which you have done. Never once did I mention to you that I expected you to move it. Your task was to push. And now you come to me, with your strength spent, thinking you have failed. But is that really so? Look at yourself. Your arms are strong and muscled, your back is sinewy and brown, your hands are calloused from constant pressure, and your legs have become massive and hard. Through opposition, you have grown much, and your abilities now surpass that which you used to have. You haven't moved the rock, but your calling was to be obedient and to push and to exercise your faith and trust in my wisdom. This you have done. I, your friend, will now move the rock."

Believe God is at work developing you. Persevere. Someone put it this way: when life is in a lull, just PUSH: Persevere Until Something Happens. When everything seems to go wrong, when nothing works out the way you had planned, when the dreams seem to crash, push. When the job gets you down, when people don't react or treat you the way you think they should, when people don't understand you, push until something happens. It's the first attitude you need to get ready for promotion.

The second attitude to glean from Joseph's imprisonment is to raise your perspective. I once read that a head hung in despair cannot see the horizon of God's provision. How true! Look up and change your horizon. The cupbearer remembered Joseph's ability to interpret dreams, so Pharaoh sent for Joseph, who ultimately interpreted the dreams. Why was Joseph ready for this opportunity? The answer is in verses 38–39: "Pharaoh asked them, 'Can we find anyone like this man, one in whom is the spirit of God?' Then Pharaoh said to Joseph, 'Since God has made all this known to you, there is no one so discerning and wise as you.'" Because he had made God his horizon, Joseph was wise and discerning. He had shrewd, God-given insight and acted accordingly. Familiarity with God and His ways enabled Joseph to be discerning. He knew, as Proverbs 21:1 states, "In the LORD's hand the king's heart is a stream of water that he channels toward all who please him." So when Pharaoh called for him, Joseph knew God was ready to act in a powerful way. As a godly person, Joseph had insight that the worldly rulers and interpreters didn't have.

If you put a buzzard in a pen six feet by eight feet, the bird will be in prison even if the pen is completely open on top. It needs a "runway" of ten or so feet to get airborne. The bumblebee is similar. If dropped into a tumbler, it will buzz around there because it won't realize it can escape above; it will be a prisoner of its low horizon. Have you ever had your sights so low that you failed to see the upper horizon where God waits for you to take notice of Him?

If you're filled with the Spirit, you can look up and raise your horizon because through the Spirit, you can see and understand things others cannot. It doesn't mean you're more intelligent than others, just that you have an understanding of spiritual realities others don't.

> At that same time Jesus was filled with the joy of the Holy Spirit, and he said, "O Father, Lord of heaven and earth, thank you for hiding these things from those who think themselves wise and clever, and for revealing them to the childlike. Yes, Father, it pleased you to do it this way." (Luke 10:21 NLT)

God revealed the dreams to Joseph, not to Pharaoh's men; Paul explained this.

> The person without the Spirit does not accept the things that come from the Spirit of God but considers them foolishness, and cannot understand them because they are discerned only through the Spirit. The person with the Spirit makes judgments about all things, but such a person is not subject to merely human judgments, for, "Who has known the mind of the Lord so as to instruct him?" But we have the mind of Christ. (1 Corinthians 2:14–16)

While you're waiting for promotion, the world might mock you or forget you. And when God acts, they will not understand, but they will know the power and uniqueness of the Christian testimony. When you demonstrate the wisdom of God and willingly testify to and use the resources and insights God gave to you, the world will notice. Use the time of growth to learn more about God, to study His Word, and to strengthen your relationship with Jesus Christ. That will raise your horizon.

Joseph also raised his perspective by promoting God. When Pharaoh told Joseph he had some dreams and had heard Joseph could interpret them, Joseph responded, "I cannot do it … but God will give Pharaoh the answer he desires" (v. 16).

For many years, I thought people who deferred credit to God were just being flippant, overly pious, and maybe insincerely humble. But Father, forgive me; I've learned that even though that's true of some, many others sincerely mean it and are truly humble in doing so. Perhaps they learned it from Joseph, who willingly and boldly gave God the credit. This wasn't a one-time testimony by Joseph. Verses 50–52 tell us the names of his two sons. One, Manasseh, means *to forget misery*, and the other, Ephraim, means *twice fruitful in the land of his affliction*. Their names bore testimony to Joseph's faith in God. He gave credit where it was due.

Think again about Paul Glock's choice. His story, like all the stories of martyrs' imprisonments, are not at all like Hollywood movies. Imprisoned martyrs don't invent ways to escape; there's no plan for rescue. Martyrs like Paul Glock don't escape even when they have the chance. Rather, their choice is to use every situation for God's glory regardless of their circumstances. Perhaps they learned from Paul and Silas who, precisely because they chose not to escape jail, had the opportunity to lead their jailer and his family to Christ.

When you feel imprisoned and restrained, what choice do you make? Do you focus on finding a way out of your troubles, or do you focus on the fact you might be exactly where God wants you to be? God often wants endurance rather than escape. When feeling imprisoned, raise your horizon and give credit where credit is due—promote God.

The third attitude in getting ready for promotion is to relish reward— anticipate promotion. Verses 40 and following tell us that Joseph was richly rewarded for his waiting; he went from the pit to the prison and then to the palace. Pharaoh conferred status and honor on him. Pharaoh made him in essence prime minister, comptroller, and chief justice. He told Joseph, "I am Pharaoh, but without your word no one will lift hand or foot in all of Egypt" (41:44). He conferred honor and authority on Joseph. He gave him his official signet ring, told him to ride in the second chariot, and ordered people to bow to him; he gave him a new name and a royal wife. As Paul wrote years later to Timothy, "For physical training is of some value, but godliness has value for all things, holding promise for both the present life and the life to come" (1 Timothy 4:8). Jesus similarly promised, "But seek first his kingdom and his righteousness, and all these things will be given to you as well" (Matthew 6:33).

Joseph relished his reward as he rejoiced in God. I mentioned that the names of his sons were expressions of faith in God, but they were also expressions of thanks to God. Even as Joseph was exalted, so he exalted God. This chapter turns the focus from the failures and frustrations of

Joseph to the faithfulness of God. God's faithfulness allows you to rejoice in all circumstances. The prophet Isaiah wrote,

> Can a mother forget the baby at her breast and have no compassion on the child she has borne? Though she may forget, I will not forget you! See, I have engraved you on the palms of my hands; your walls are ever before me. (Isaiah 49:15–16)

In the midst of his laments, Jeremiah wrote,

> Because of the LORD's great love we are not consumed, for his compassions never fail. They are new every morning; great is your faithfulness. I say to myself, "The LORD is my portion; therefore I will wait for him." The LORD is good to those whose hope is in him, to the one who seeks him; it is good to wait quietly for the salvation of the LORD. (Jeremiah 3:22–26).

You can rejoice because you know, in the words of Paul.

> He who began a good work in you will carry it on to completion until the day of Christ Jesus. (Philippians 1:6)

God is faithful. You can rejoice because it's God's pattern and purpose to exalt His people as He exalted His Son. As Joseph was exalted to the right hand of Pharaoh, so Jesus was exalted to the right hand of God. As Joseph was given authority to rule Egypt, so Jesus was given authority to rule the nations as the "King of kings and Lord of lords." All citizens were commanded to bow to Joseph.

> At the name of Jesus every knee should bow, in heaven and on earth and under the earth, and every tongue confess that Jesus Christ is Lord, to the glory of God the Father. (Philippians 2:11)

You will be exalted too.

Paul wrote,

Therefore I endure everything for the sake of the elect, that they too may obtain the salvation that is in Christ Jesus, with eternal glory ... if we endure, we will also reign with him. (2 Timothy 2:10–12)

John began the final chapter of Revelation this way.

Then the angel showed me the river of the water of life, as clear as crystal, flowing from the throne of God and of the Lamb down the middle of the great street of the city. On each side of the river stood the tree of life, bearing twelve crops of fruit, yielding its fruit every month. And the leaves of the tree are for the healing of the nations. No longer will there be any curse. The throne of God and of the Lamb will be in the city, and his servants will serve him. They will see his face, and his name will be on their foreheads. There will be no more night. They will not need the light of a lamp or the light of the sun, for the Lord God will give them light. And they will reign for ever and ever. (Revelation 22:1–5)

This is your future. God is preparing you for promotion. Are you preparing yourself? Are you living in the hope of your glorious future? Do you trust the promises of God?

Joe Bayly and his wife had seven children but lost all three of their sons at different ages and to different circumstances. One died of leukemia before he was five. The despair and grief were overwhelming, but their faith eventually triumphed, and he wrote powerfully of his journey and his testimony.

One Saturday morning in January, I saw the mail truck stop at our mailbox up on the road. Without thinking, except that I wanted to get the mail, I ran out of the house and up the road in my shirt sleeves. It was bitterly cold – the temperature was below zero—there was a brisk wind from the north, and the ground was covered with more than a foot of snow. I opened the mailbox, pulled out the mail, and was about to make a mad dash for the house when I saw what was on the bottom, under the letters: a Burpee seed catalog.

On the front were bright zinnias. I turned it over. On the back were huge tomatoes. For a few moments I was oblivious to the cold, delivered from it. I leafed through the catalog, tasting corm and cucumbers, smelling roses. I was the freshly plowed earth, smelled it, let it run through my fingers. For those brief moments, I was living in the springtime and summer, winter past. Then the cold penetrated to my bones and I ran back to the house.

When the door was closed behind me, and I was getting warm again, I thought how my moments at the mailbox were like our experience as Christians. We feel the cold, along with those who do not share our hope. The biting wind penetrates us as them …

But in our cold times, we have a seed catalog. We open it and smell the promised spring, eternal spring. And the firstfruit that settles our hope is Jesus Christ, who was raised from death and cold to glory eternal.[40]

Do you trust the promises, the eternal spring of God? Do you believe that all His promises find their "Yes" in Jesus (2 Corinthians 1:20)?

Back once more to Paul Glock. Though his choice was to remain in prison even if it meant death for Christ, God later chose to promote and honor Paul apart from martyrdom. In 1576, a fire broke out in the castle where he was held. He and a fellow prisoner helped put out the flames and so won their freedom before the religious leaders, who staunchly opposed Paul, could revoke it. Our lives are constantly advancing toward the completion of God's plan for us. You're always preparing for promotion. Do you trust God's promises?

During my freshman year in college when I felt so restrained and imprisoned, God woke me up one morning and led me to write a letter to my parents saying I was going into the ministry. No flashes of lightning, no loud voices, no tap on the shoulder, just an inner conviction that this was why I had been imprisoned and restrained. God was getting my attention and getting me ready for promotion; He had much higher aspirations for me than I had for myself. Our lives are constantly advancing toward the completion of God's plan for us. We're always getting ready for promotion.

Even in your life's prisons, even during your dreariest hours, God is with you and at work in, through, and around you. God will always exalt you, so turn your depressing prison into grand promotion. Even in the midst of his dire laments, the prophet Jeremiah could say,

> The LORD is good to those whose hope is in him, to the one who seeks him; it is good to wait quietly for the salvation of the LORD. (Lamentations 3:25–26)

Say it aloud even if the person next to you will hear you—especially if the person next to you will hear you: "The LORD is my portion; therefore I will wait for him." (Lamentations 3:24)

For Your Reflection

There's an old legend about a weary traveler reaching the Mississippi River for the first time. There was no bridge. It was early winter, and the river had iced over, but he didn't know if it could bear his weight. Night was falling; it was urgent he get to the other side. Finally, after much hesitation and with great fear, he began to crawl across the ice, trying to distribute his weight. About halfway across, he heard singing behind him. Out of the dusk came a man driving a wagon full of coal across the river and singing lustily. One was crawling while the other was just about flying across the same ice.

Too often, we crawl rather than walk in the promises of God. God has promised to be with us, uphold us, and grant us victory over our spiritual enemies, so we can stand and walk to His heavenly home. In the words of R. Kelso Carter,

Standing on the promises of Christ my king,
Through eternal ages let His praises ring,
Glory in the highest, I will shout and sing,
Standing on the promises of God.

Standing on the promises that cannot fail,
When the howling storms of doubt and fear assail,
By the living Word of God I shall prevail,
Standing on the promises of God.

Standing on the promises I now can see
Perfect, present cleansing in the blood for me;
Standing in the liberty where Christ makes free,
Standing on the promises of God.

Standing on the promises of Christ the Lord,
Bound to Him eternally by love's strong cord,
Overcoming daily with the Spirit's sword,
Standing on the promises of God.

Standing on the promises I cannot fall,
Listening every moment to the Spirit's call
Resting in my Savior as my all in all,
Standing on the promises of God.

Standing, standing,
Standing on the promises of God my Savior;
Standing, standing,
I'm standing on the promises of God.

CHAPTER 6

When the Going Gets Tough …
Pity Parties Become Professions of Faith

Genesis 42:1–38

The money is found

Pity: a cause for regret or disappointment; feel sorrow for the misfortunes of.

Have you ever felt sorry for yourself and hosted your own pity party? One
Saturday early in my ministry was my birthday. I'd planned to take the

day off and enjoy it; my wife, Barb, and I were going out for supper that night—at that time, a real treat.

But the phone rang. A young wife was in despair about her marriage. I swallowed hard and went to see her. It took much longer than I had expected, and since she was going to be confronting her husband momentarily, I had a feeling I'd be back. So my return home was the start of my pity party. *Poor me. I can't even get a day off. I can't even enjoy my own birthday. It just isn't fair!* I wasn't very pleasant to be around.

It wasn't long before I headed back to the young wife. I later returned to see her for a third time. By the time I returned home after that third visit, I wasn't a happy camper. I'd never felt so sorry for myself. As I walked through the backdoor, I told Barb that I didn't feel like going out and that it was too late to do so anyway, and then I started in on the whole "pity me" routine. I didn't know that in our living room were friends waiting to surprise me for my birthday. In my pitiful mood, I hadn't seen any signs and almost destroyed what Barb had worked so hard to pull off. Ever been there and done that? Very little if any good grows out of self-pity.

Genesis 42 powerfully portrays the consequences of self-pity. The last time we read of Joseph's family, his brothers had deceived their father and led him to believe Joseph was dead. Since then, the focus has been on Joseph and God's goodness to him. Now we return to his family and discover the consequences of self-pity. The first consequence is that they had deadened consciences. The sons had lived for over twenty years knowing what they had done to Joseph and how they were daily deceiving their father. They lived with the fact that their jealousy and self-pity because of Joseph's favored status had led them to commit an evil deed, but they were also increasingly comfortable with the passage of time. We slowly grow accustomed to our sinful deeds and become numb to sin. Then it slowly destroys us.

Dr. George Sweeting wrote of an experience with his family.

> Several years ago our family visited Niagara Falls. It was spring, and ice was rushing down the river. As I viewed the large blocks of ice flowing toward the falls, I could see that there were carcasses of dead fish embedded in the ice. Gulls by the score were riding down the river feeding on the fish. As they

came to the brink of the falls, their wings would go out, and they would escape from the falls. I watched one gull which seemed to delay and wondered when it would leave. It was engrossed in the carcass of a fish, and when it finally came to the brink of the falls, out went its powerful wings. The bird flapped and flapped and even lifted the ice out of the water, and I thought it would escape. But it had delayed too long so that its claws had frozen into the ice. The weight of the ice was too great, and the gull plunged into the abyss.[41]

Are you feasting on the carcass of some sin, your conscience deadened, unaware of the coming falls? The longer you live with the carcass of your sins, the more numb you become to them.

We see the second characteristic of a deadened conscience in that the brothers were prone to inaction. At some point, our deadened consciences cause our minds to freeze up; we become so overwhelmed with self-pity that the flow of our normal creative juices is stopped. Look at verse 1, in which Jacob said to his sons, "Why do you just keep looking at each other?" They were low on food, but their minds were so muddled they could only stare at each other. They had become blind to solutions, oblivious of possibilities, and had no imagination, no energy, no desire to do anything. They were pouting children who didn't want to do anything but feel sorry for themselves.

Ever felt stuck in neutral, oblivious of possibilities? Too emotionally lethargic to do anything? Feel your imagination was dead? Unless there's a physical cause (always worth checking out), it could well be a sign that your conscience is dead or dying. Take some time to look at your life; look for some sinful deed you've never dealt with or confessed, a sin that might well be weighing heavily on your conscience without your being aware of it anymore.

When I kept silent, my bones wasted away through my groaning all day long. For day and night your hand was heavy on me; my strength was sapped as in the heat of summer. (Psalm 32:3–4)

As Eugene Peterson translated verse 4 (*The Message*), "The pressure never let up; all the juices of my life dried up." Ever identified with that? Don't miss the psalmist's solution: "Then I acknowledged my sin to you and did not cover up my iniquity. I said, 'I will confess my transgressions to the LORD.' And you forgave the guilt of my sin" (Psalm 32:5).

Third, with a deadened conscience, the brothers discovered that doing the common became difficult. In verse 2, Jacob told the brothers to buy grain in Egypt. While it would be a long journey, it was not too much to ask of these grown men. But at the mention of Egypt, they knew they had to retrace their shameful steps and revisit that haunting site where they had gotten rid of Joseph. They would have to relive their sinful, shameful past.

There was a scary intersection near a church I served. Twice during my years there, I was broadsided at that intersection by drivers who ran red lights. To this day, I cannot go through that intersection without slowing down and taking an extra look; I remember whether I want to or not. The brothers would pass through the intersection of their sinful deeds and would remember whether they wanted to or not. It would be a difficult journey.

What intersection, scene, place, experience, or journey would be difficult for you to revisit? What, try as you will, can you not forget? What are you doing about it?

The brothers were also haunted by retribution.

> They said to one another, "Surely we are being punished because of our brother. We saw how distressed he was when he pleaded with us for his life, but we would not listen; that's why this distress has come upon us." (vv. 21–23)

The root of the Hebrew word for *distress* means "to bind, to restrict, to cramp, to tie up." The brothers acknowledged that their stomachs were in knots because they were sure they would be punished for their sin. There's no pain greater than a troubled conscience. Sir Robert Watson-Watt helped invent radar. Years later, much to his chagrin, he was driving in Canada and was arrested for speeding—after being timed by his own radar! He later wrote a short verse: "Pity Sir Robert Watson-Watt, strange target of his radar plot. And thus with others I could mention, a victim of his own invention." The brothers were convinced they were about to be the victims of their own evil actions.

It's not pleasant to live in expectation of punishment for something you've done. The words "Go to your room until I come up there!" or "Just wait until your father gets home!" are so powerful because they produce distress at the thought of coming punishment. Have you ever felt God was punishing you for something you'd done? What was it, and how did you feel God was punishing you? Were you ever the victim of your own evil actions—your sin—in some other way?

Self-pity produces a deadened conscience, which in turn produces numbness to sin, proneness to inaction, a sense that the common has become difficult, and a haunting expectation of retribution.

While a deadened conscience is one consequence of self-pity, another is a distorted conscience. "Reuben replied, 'Didn't I tell you not to sin against the boy? But you wouldn't listen! Now we must give an accounting for his blood'" (v. 24). The flow of grace was blocked by guilt. The brothers' guilt led them to see God only in terms of judgment. This was the first time they mentioned God, and it was because they feared His judgment. When they found the money in the sack, they were sure it was a trap; they didn't consider it might be a sign of favor and grace. As Matthew Henry put it, "Guilty consciences are apt to take good providences in a bad sense, and to put wrong constructions even upon those things that make (good) for them. They flee when none pursues."[42] Receiving the gift of grace can be blocked by guilt.

Has anything ever happened to you that led you to think God was punishing or tempting you? What caused you to feel that way? Because you viewed God more as a judge than a grace giver? What if anything changed your view? Was God in fact doing something good or beneficial? Receiving the gift of grace can be blocked by guilt.

The narrative continues.

> Joseph gave orders to fill their bags with grain, to put each man's silver back in his sack, and to give them provisions for their journey. After this was done for them, they loaded their grain on their donkeys and left. At the place where they

stopped for the night one of them opened his sack to get feed for his donkey, and he saw his silver in the mouth of his sack. "My silver has been returned," he said to his brothers. "Here it is in my sack." Their hearts sank and they turned to each other trembling and said, "What is this that God has done to us?" (vv. 25–28)

The word for *trembling* is used in 1 Samuel 14:15 to describe a giant earthquake. With grace blocked by guilt, everything they did and thought from that point was from the perspective of fear and caused them to tremble greatly.

Nothing is more destructive to peace of mind and sound decision making than fear, which stifles us. Remember Adam and Eve: "Then the man and his wife heard the sound of the LORD God as he was walking in the garden in the cool of the day, and they hid from the LORD God among the trees of the garden" (Genesis 3:8). Just after God pronounced punishment upon Cain for killing his brother, "Cain said to the LORD, 'My punishment is more than I can bear. Today you are driving me from the land, and I will be hidden from your presence; I will be a restless wanderer on the earth, and whoever finds me will kill me'" (Genesis 4:13-14).

Fear is the darkroom where negatives are developed. It stifles us. It haunts us. Have you ever been fearful? Perhaps you were all alone, or in the dark, or had a sense someone was following you. It's haunting, isn't it? I remember the first time I stayed in a beautiful prayer retreat cottage that since has become very precious to me. It's in a larger camp but separate from the rest of the facilities and population. It sits in some majestic woods by a small, serene, private lake. There are no curtains over the windows of the small kitchen or front door. For a while, I kept looking over my shoulder at those windows; fear was playing mind games with me. I felt someone might be peering in at me. Odd, isn't it? I was in a prayer cottage but was for a brief time haunted by fear. Similarly, Joseph's brothers were fearful. They kept looking over their shoulders, haunted by the sense that someone was following them, peering at them, out to get them. They were haunted by the sense of being watched and hunted.

An Arab chief told a story of a spy captured and sentenced to death by a general in the Persian army. This general had the strange custom of giving condemned criminals a choice between the firing squad and "the big, black door." As the moment for execution drew near, the guards brought the spy to the general. "What will it be," asked the general, "the firing squad or the big, black door?" The spy hesitated for a long time before choosing the firing squad. A few minutes later, shots confirmed the spy's execution. The general told his aide, "They always prefer the known to the unknown. People fear what they don't know. Yet we gave him a choice." The aide asked, "What lies beyond the big door?" The general replied, "Freedom. I've only known a few brave enough to take that door."

A distorted conscience results in guilt blocking grace and fear stifling us, and that leads to distrustful consciences.

> As they were emptying their sacks, there in each man's sack was his pouch of silver! When they and their father saw the money pouches, they were frightened. Their father Jacob said to them, "You have deprived me of my children. Joseph is no more and Simeon is no more, and now you want to take Benjamin. Everything is against me!" (vv. 35–36)

Jacob no longer trusted his sons or God. He had forgotten the God who promised, "I am with you and will keep you wherever you go." When trust disappears, we begin to look at everyone and everything with suspicion and distrust.

A poor widow faced eviction. She was behind in her rent and other bills, her power had been cut off, and she had received an eviction notice. One day, she heard a knock on the door. She sat trembling in silence behind locked doors and drawn curtains. There was another knock, and again she sat frozen in fear that officials had come to kick her out. Finally, the knocking stopped, and she was able to relax a little bit. If only she had answered the knock, she would have been greeted by her pastor, who had worked together with friends to collect enough to pay her rent and bills. He had come with relief, but her fear and distrust blocked the good news. Self-pity creates a deadened, distorted, distrustful conscience that makes us miss great opportunities.

But enough about the consequences of self-pity. The question is, how do you move beyond it? With a counterattack of faith. You attack self-pity by activating at least two elements of faith. First, your profession of faith. It's nice to believe, as I've been saying throughout this book, that God is in all the events of our lives, and we have little problem with that during blessed and glorious events. But it's much tougher to swallow and accept under the bitterness of trial and tough times. The apostle Paul is a great example. Even as he sat in prison awaiting word of his fate, he said,

> Rejoice in the Lord always. I will say it again: Rejoice! Let your gentleness be evident to all. The Lord is near [at hand]. Do not be anxious about anything, but in everything, by prayer and petition, with thanksgiving, present your requests to God. (Philippians 4:4–6)

No matter what the trial, no matter how bleak the outlook, no matter how confining the prison, the Lord is at hand. Turn your pity party into a profession of faith. It's precisely what Joseph did. Verse 6 says he became governor of the land. Though he had been sold by his brothers, worked as a slave, and spent time in prison, he was in a good position when his brothers came for food. The Lord was at hand. Imagine how Joseph felt when he recognized his brothers and they—not recognizing him—bowed to him! "Then he remembered his dreams about them" (v. 9). He realized his divine dreams were being fulfilled. The Lord was at hand. God needed his family in Egypt, and he was about to move them there. Joseph's faith reached new heights, and everything he did from that moment on was done from that faith. Everything he was about to do was part of professing his faith.

So often, we wait for God to do some fantastic, obvious, miraculous thing in our lives when in reality He is constantly at work and at hand. But His providence is most often seen and understood only in hindsight. God works that way to get us to walk by faith, not sight. Notice the contrast in Joseph's family; Joseph mentioned God frequently and therefore saw Him at work all the time; his family seldom mentioned God and failed to see Him; they could only fear Him. They were stuck at a pity party.

But it's not necessary to be stuck. J. I. Packer, one of the most influential Christian theologians of the modern era, said blindness was forcing him to step down from his extensive speaking and writing ministry. His macular degeneration led to such a loss of vision that he is unable to read or write. Packer, eighty-nine, says he will no longer do regular preaching or traveling. "God knows what He's doing," Packer told the Gospel Coalition. "This comes as a clear indication from headquarters and I take it from Him." In the interview, Packer also spoke of Ecclesiastes, one of his favorite books. "The author of Ecclesiastes has taught me that it is folly to suppose that you can plan life and master it, and you will get hurt if you try," he said. "You must acknowledge the sovereignty of God and leave the wisdom to Him."[43] Packer could have chosen a pity party; but he chose a profession of faith. He will walk by faith, not by sight.

This profession of faith also teaches us we should judge nothing before its time. Again, consider Joseph's family. His brothers scoffed at the dreams of bowing to Joseph, but they were bowing to him. They had accused him of spying on them, but he would accuse them of spying. They had put him in a pit, and he had been enslaved and imprisoned, but they would be enslaved to him and one of them imprisoned. They had shown no mercy and were sure they would receive none.

Judge nothing before its time. Don't let the pain of the process obscure the fact of healing. The pain of surgery must not overrule the healing brought about by the surgery. Time will show the wisdom of the surgery. We often cannot understand the ways of God until we can see the whole picture. Give God a chance.

Turning your pity party into your profession of faith will activate the power of Christ. Remember Jacob's words as he sent his sons to Egypt: "Go down there and buy some for us, so that we may live and not die." Joseph eventually said to them, "It was to save lives that God sent me ahead of you." In the same way, God sent Jesus ahead of us to save lives. Jesus will end the famine.

> Jesus declared, "I am the bread of life. Whoever comes to me will never go hungry, and whoever believes in me will never be thirsty ... I am the living bread that came down from heaven. Whoever eats this bread will live forever. This bread is my flesh, which I will give for the life of the world." (John 6:35, 51)

The cross of Christ is the focal point of your profession of faith. "For God so loved the world that he gave his one and only Son, that whoever believes in him shall not perish but have eternal life." The cross reminds us, "If God is for us, who can be against us? He who did not spare his own Son, but gave him up for us all—how will he not also, along with him, graciously give us all things?" (Romans 8:31–32)

After the Heidelberg Catechism teaches about God's providence, it asks the question of application: "What advantage comes from acknowledging God's creation and providence?" It offers an instructive three-part answer. The way to turn your pity party into a profession of faith is first, be patient in adversity.[44] Paul wrote, "We also rejoice in our sufferings, because we know that suffering produces perseverance; perseverance, character; and character, hope" (Romans 5:3–4). God is always growing you. Growth takes time. Be patient.

Second, be grateful in blessing. It's so much easier to complain when things go wrong than it is to be grateful when things go well. But when you're patient in adversity, you can be grateful in the midst of blessing. That's why Moses on several occasions reminded the Israelites, "You shall bless the Lord your God for the good land he has given you."

A nice young post office worker was sorting through mail when she discovered a letter addressed, "GOD, c/o Heaven." The letter told about an old woman who had never asked for anything in her life. She was desperately in need of $100 and was wondering if God would send her the money. The young woman was touched enough to pass the hat, and she raised $90, which she sent to the woman. A few weeks later, another letter arrived addressed in the same way to God: "Thank you for the money, God. I deeply appreciate it. However, I received only $90. It must have been those jerks at the post office!" Been there, done that—been ungrateful for what I didn't get rather than grateful for what I received. How about you?

Once you realize through the cross the greatness of Jesus' love, your heart will be filled to overflowing with gratitude for what and Who you have, for Who has you. And the byproduct of gratitude is joy—joy doesn't lead to gratitude; it's the other way around. How have you been blessed? Where and how can you presently express more gratitude?

When we are patient in adversity and grateful in the midst of blessing, we can trust God for the future. When we believe nothing can separate us from the love of God in Christ Jesus, we replace fear with trust.

Pam, a dear friend of our family, wrote of an experience she and her daughter Jen shared.

Jen was riding the bus home from school about 4 pm and the bus crossed over the highway onto a busy street and turned into our plat. About one block in, the bus driver passed out and the bus went into a snowbank. There happened to be a sixth grader on the bus who ran up, used the bus radio to call 911 and shut off the motor to the bus and placed it in gear.

Ok, now the "Praise God" part. Across the street lived a Police officer who had just pulled in his driveway; he came running. My neighbor who is a fire fighter was coming down the street; he helped. The sixth grader knew enough to call 911 and figured out how to shut down the bus. There just happened to be a big enough snow bank in this particular part of the street that could stop the bus from running into the house a stones throw away and we are so very thankful that he was in the plat and not crossing over the highway or even on the busy street with all of the traffic.

No one was hurt and last report says that the bus driver had a heart attack and is in stable condition. Now none of the neighborhood kids want to ride the bus in fear, so they are going to have counselors at school to work with the kids. Jen said, during her prayer, "Thank you God and Daddy for keeping us safe on the bus and help our bus driver to be able to drive us again so he'll know we still love him." Me, acting like the deranged mother said, "Are you nuts? I'm sure he won't be driving school bus anymore." Jen replied, "Mom, remember we are not in control and you have to let go and trust in God that I will be safe." So, please pray that I can place my children on the bus in the morning and NOT follow it to school and then home again. Maybe I should stop and learn from my very wise daughter.

What would it mean for you to trust God more? I encourage you to reflect on your life right now. Trace the hand of God throughout it. Rediscover how He has been faithful to you and guided, protected, and molded you. It will help you trust Him.

Tommy loved to spend time with his grandparents. Grandfather was retired and was able to spend time with him. They'd go fishing, to a ballgame, to the zoo, or they would just sit around and be with each other. One day, they were sitting in the sun, fishing, when Tommy said, "Grandfather, can you see God?" His grandfather had a way of not always answering a question immediately; he'd think a bit first. That time, however, he paused for such a long time and there was such a faraway look in his eyes that Tommy thought he hadn't heard. So he asked again, "Grandfather, can you see God?" Grandfather replied softly, "Tommy, it's getting so lately that I don't see much of anything else." When your next pity part starts, profess and activate your faith; look at the cross of Jesus Christ. Begin right now praying that whatever the circumstances, you don't see much of anything else.

For Your Reflection

(inspired by Nehemiah 9:16 and Psalm 77:11, 12)

> We will remember, we will remember
> We will remember the works of Your hands
> We will stop and give you praise
> For great is Thy faithfulness
>
> You're our creator, our life sustainer
> Deliverer, our comfort, our joy
> Throughout the ages You've been our shelter
> Our peace in the midst of the storm

With signs and wonders You've shown Your power
With precious blood You showed us Your grace
You've been our helper, our liberator
The giver of life with no end

We will remember, we will remember
We will remember the works of Your hands
We will stop and give you praise
For great is Thy faithfulness

When we walk through life's darkest valleys
We will look back at all You have done
And we will shout, our God is good
And He is the faithful One

Bridge:
Hallelujah, hallelujah
To the one from whom all blessings flow
Hallelujah, hallelujah
To the one whose glory has been shown

We will remember, we will remember
We will remember the works of Your hands
We will stop and give you praise
For great is Thy faithfulness

I still remember the day You saved me
The day I heard You call out my name
You said You loved me and would never leave me
And I've never been the same

We will remember, we will remember
We will remember the works of Your hands
We will stop and give you praise
For great is Thy faithfulness[45]

CHAPTER 7

When the Going Gets Tough ...
Guilt Becomes Gift

Genesis 43:1–44:34

The cup is found in the sack

*Guilt: the fact of having committed a specified or implied offense or
crime; a feeling of having done wrong or failed in an obligation.*

A deputy district attorney asked several robbery victims to study a lineup
of five people. He'd placed the suspect in the middle and told each man to
step forward and say, "Give me all your money—and I need some change

in quarters and dimes." The first man stepped forward and said, "Give me all your money—and I need some change in quarters and dimes." The second man did the same. Then the suspect stepped forward and blurted out, "That's not what I said!"

Isn't it amazing how guilt influences our behavior? Genesis 43–44 portrays guilt at work in Joseph's brothers. So a good starting point is to analyze the character of guilt, which comes in two types. First, there is a *sense* of guilt; the technical term is false guilt. At its primary level, it's like children reciting the old saying, "Step on a crack and you'll break your mother's back." Suppose I had as a child said that one day as I stepped on a crack in the sidewalk and the next day my mother had fallen and broken her back. I would have been horror stricken at the thought it was all my fault. That's false guilt—feeling guilty when there's no reason.

I remember the first time I smoked. My uncle had tossed a partially smoked cigarette in his backyard and went inside. I was alone, looked around, picked it up, and took a puff. *Yuck! This tastes terrible!* I had an overwhelming sense of guilt, but it was false guilt.

Many fine parents have done wonderful jobs of raising their children yet have suffered as one of their offspring went astray or wandered from the fold; the parents think, *It's our fault. If we had loved her more, disciplined her more, this wouldn't have happened!* While in some cases that could be true, in many it isn't. It's false guilt.

Far too many children experience the divorce of their parents and blame themselves for their parents' divorce. That's false guilt.

A minister once said that two women in his church had died and the funerals were on successive days. The women had lived long, full lives. The son of one said to the clergyman, "I should have sent my mother to Florida, where the sun is shining and warm. This cold, miserable winter weather is the cause of her death. I feel guilty for not sending her south." The next day, the other woman's son said to the clergyman, "I shouldn't have sent my mother to Florida this winter. The change in climate and the long plane ride and being away from familiar things killed her. I feel guilty about that." That's all false guilt.

Dr. Paul Brand pointed out that false guilt was like phantom limb pain. This pain occurs in some people after an amputation. Even though a limb is amputated, some amputees feel pain, phantom pain but real pain, where the amputated limb once was. So it is with false guilt; there's no guilt, but the pain of guilt is real.

There's also real guilt. God banished Cain, and Cain complained he couldn't bear the punishment. In 2 Samuel 24, David went against the command of God and counted his fighting men. Verse 10 states, "David was conscience-stricken after he had counted the fighting men, and he said to the Lord, 'I have sinned.'" That's real guilt at work. Judas betrayed Jesus and hung himself; that's real guilt at work.

The wise man wrote, "The wicked are edgy with guilt, ready to run off even when no one's after them" (Proverbs 28:1 MSG).

Real guilt is ascribed by God when we violate his will. When I was young, my family lived half a block from a neighborhood grocery store where we ran a tab. One day, I decided I wanted some candy, so I went to the store and put it on our bill. I went through it so fast that I went back and got some more, telling the owner some story about needing it for friends or a party. She put it on our bill. That time, I went straight home and ran under our front porch to hide while I ate it. We have built-in sensors that trigger alarms when we violate God's will; they go off when we cross the line established by God's law. That's real guilt.

Jacob's sons experienced this guilt. Judah said, "God has uncovered your servants' guilt" (44:16). Their deceit had come to the surface. Similarly Cathleen Crowell Webb knew the truth of guilt all too well. On a July night in 1977, she was picked up by the police. She was a frightened, confused sixteen-year-old with a ripped blouse and a face smudged by tears. She sobbed out the story that she had been raped. Police later arrested Gary Dotson, who matched Cathleen's description of her attacker. Her testimony led to his conviction and a twenty- to twenty-five-year sentence. In 1985, Cathleen was married and the mother of two. She went back to court to recant her testimony. She had made up the rape story because of fear she was pregnant by her boyfriend and didn't want her foster parents to find out. The judge refused to believe her, stating she couldn't be trusted. But she explained it all this way.

Once I made my decision to become a Christian, I felt at peace. It is an abundant joy and a peace that passes all understanding. I was praising God for all the sins he had forgiven me for. I was listing all my sins in my mind and then I came to this one about the lie. For the first time I faced the fact that I had done something so horrible and I needed to make restitution for it. But there was no way I was going to do that. I started listing all the consequences—maybe my husband would hate me, maybe he would leave me. I thought the whole world would hate me. I decided there was no way I was going to come forward. Basically I was being disobedient to God's commandments. The guilt kept building up and building up over three and a half years until I couldn't take it anymore. I'd cry in the middle of the day and I'd look at my infant son and think, how would I feel if my son were in jail? So, finally, I told the pastor's wife about my lie, and she told the pastor. I told my husband the next day. I knew he loved me, but I felt it was going to hurt the trust we had between each other. But he said, "Cathy, you have to do the right thing." He has been totally supportive. Since then we've grown closer, not further apart.

I realized that after I informed the first person about my false cry of rape, that the wheels couldn't stop until Gary Dotson was freed. Obviously this confession was no longer something I could keep secret. Besides, it is a Biblical principle that if you defame a person publicly, you must restore him publicly. I then authorized my attorney, John J. McLario of Menomonee Falls, Wis., a friend of my pastor, to represent me as I came forward and made the truth public.[46]

That's real guilt at work.

Researchers at the University of Toronto published data in 2006 that suggested people experience "a powerful urge to wash themselves" when suffering from a guilty conscience. This urge is known as the Macbeth effect, referring to Shakespeare's famous play in which one of the main characters cries, "Out, damned spot!" while trying to scrub away bloodstains that exist only in her mind. To study this effect, the researchers asked volunteers to think about immoral acts they had committed in the past—shoplifting, betraying a friend, and so on. The volunteers were then offered an opportunity to clean their hands. According to the study, those who had retraced their sins "jumped at the offer at twice the rate of study subjects who had not imagined past transgressions."[47] That's real guilt at work.

But whether guilt is false or real, it has some basic, destructive traits. The first is that it leads to self-punishing behavior. Plato once said, "The soul will run eagerly to its judge." Consider Larry, who had served two terms in San Quentin for theft and forgery. When he was released after his second term, he went on another check-kiting spree and even signed his own name to the checks, which made it ridiculously easy to trace him. He was sentenced to a third term.

We have an inner mechanism that enforces the principle "confess or be punished." We confess, or find a way to be punished, or punish ourselves. Larry was saying in essence, "I'm still guilty. Find me and punish me." Police tell us criminals often want the attention and even leave obvious clues because they want to be caught.

The second destructive trait of guilt is fear. Since we considered fear in the last chapter, I'll add just one more dimension of fear here. There's a story that claims Sir Arthur Conan Doyle played a practical joke on twelve of his friends; he sent them telegrams that read, "Flee at once ... all is discovered." Within twenty-four hours, all twelve had left the country.[48] Guilt produces fear. These two chapters of Genesis show Jacob's sons filled with fear produced by guilt. The sons were sure they were being punished for their cruel deeds and deceit, so they feared going back to Egypt without Benjamin. When they got to Egypt and again met with Joseph—still not recognizing him—they were frightened to be taken aside to Joseph's house. Instead of seeing grace, they saw trouble. Many people who have a negative view of God are in reality suffering from guilt. They haven't discovered the God of grace. Guilt-produced fear is also the reason some people start staying away from church—the presence of God triggers their guilt, and they fear God.

A third destructive trait of guilt is brokenness. The body breaks down. The story goes that European explorers of Africa discovered a strange but effective test for truth. Following any serious crime, all villagers were questioned by the witch doctor. If no one confessed, every suspect lined up to witness a spear point heated until it glowed white-hot. The test was simple. Every suspect stuck out his tongue to be touched by the hot metal. They believed that only a tongue that had told untruth would be burned. In most cases, the guilty person would bolt and run into the bushes as the spear approached. If no one ran, the test still worked. Down the line, the hot spear touched tongues without effect until the guilty person screamed in pain.

We now know that a normal tongue has enough moisture to prevent a quick burn. However, anyone under intense strain such as guilt or apprehension generally has a dry mouth and thus dry tongue. Since everyone trusted the results of the test, the innocent suspects relaxed, but the guilty suspect grew more anxious until his tongue betrayed him. Our physical bodies reveal guilt. Lie detectors operate on the same principle, measuring heart rate, blood pressure, and other physical signs of stress.

Now we can understand why David said,

> When I kept silent my bones wasted away through my groaning all day long. For day and night your hand was heavy upon me; my strength was sapped as in the heat of summer. (Psalm 32)

> My bones have no soundness because of my sin. My guilt has overwhelmed me like a burden too heavy to bear. My wounds fester and are loathsome because of my sinful folly. (Psalm 38)

I've often witnessed people in the middle of affairs become ill and experience deteriorating health. It's not just coincidence; there's a strong connection between guilt and health.

In his play *The Flies*, Jean-Paul Sartre gave a graphic description of guilt's burden.

> You will think you are leaving it behind, but it will always remain as heavy as before … Always it will be there, a dead weight holding you back … And nothing remains for you but to drag your crime after you until you die.[49]

Was he right? Yes and no. He was right in his description of the burden of guilt but wrong in his conviction that there was no relief because there is a cure for guilt. Despite the pain of allowing Benjamin to go to Egypt with his brothers, Jacob had one hope: "And may God Almighty grant you mercy before the man so that he will let your other brother and Benjamin come back with you" (43:14). His one hope was for the gift of mercy. Guilt can become a gift; it can cure and change your life for the better forever.

But how do you turn it into a gift? The first step is repentance. Remember the research about hand washing? Repentance is stepping up and washing your hands. Remember my candy purchases? The store owner figured something was up and called my mother to see if she knew I was buying candy. Once Mom knew, I needed to repent. The point of all Joseph's testing of his brothers was to see if they were sorry only because they'd been exposed for their deeds or if they had truly changed. Would they protect Benjamin or quickly give him up? Would they admit their evil deed and wash up?

Understand that repentance is more than saying, "I'm sorry." You have truly repented only when you have changed your direction and heart. Once Cathleen Crowell Webb was convicted by her God-given guilt, she did what was right. Here's an update to her story: She and her lawyer kept pursuing Gary Dotson's release. On May 13, 1985, Gov. James Thompson said although he believed Cathleen Crowell Webb had been raped and Gary Dotson had been her attacker, he invoked "mercy and compassion" and commuted Dotson's sentence to the six years he had served. It happened because Cathleen exhibited true repentance.

Remember also that forgiveness cannot be bought. It's noteworthy that Jacob finally relented and let his sons take Benjamin with them on their return to Egypt; but as he did, he gave them a stack of gifts to appease the ruler. He figured nothing was free; favor had to be bought. And Jacob was not alone. Consider the death of Pope John Paul II. Rogers Cadenhead, a self-described domain hoarder, registered www.BenedictXVI.com before the new pope's name was announced. Cadenhead secured it before Rome knew it needed it; he knew the right domain name could prove lucrative. Another name, PopeBenedictXVI.com, surpassed $16,000 on eBay. Cadenhead, however, didn't want money. He did want something in return though. In exchange for the name, Cadenhead sought "one of those hats," a free stay at the Vatican hotel, and complete absolution, no questions asked, for the third week of March 1987. Something happened during that third week that had burdened him enough that he wanted to become free of guilt. He wanted to make an exchange for forgiveness.

Ever have such a week or deed in your life? Are you really much different? Or do you want to pay your own way? Do you find yourself not wanting to be dependent on or indebted to anyone? But forgiveness cannot be purchased; it comes only through repentance. Guilt is an invitation to repent and receive the gift of grace.

The second step to turn your guilt into a gift is dealing with the source of your sin. Two farmers were fascinated by a booth at the fair where little celluloid balls bobbed on top of water jets. Customers were offered substantial prizes if they succeeded in shooting any ball off its perch. One farmer spent six quarters in a vain effort to pick off a ball. Finally, his friend pushed him aside and picked up the rifle. "Watch how I do it." He took a single shot and all six balls disappeared. The other man was amazed. "How did you do that?" The winner, laden with prizes, said, "I shot the man working the pump." You need to shoot the forces pumping out your guilt. Repent, turn, and face the future differently. Give up the memory and pain of your sin. See your guilt as an invitation to a grace-filled life.

To do that, however, you must have a representative. In Genesis 44:18, Jacob's son, Judah, approached Joseph and spoke eloquently about Jacob's sad state of affairs and how he had put himself in position to bear the blame. Out of his great compassion and love for his father, Judah was standing in the place of all his brothers at the confessional; he was willing to bear the guilt and take the blame. The good news is there is one who stands in your place. Jesus Christ is your representative. He has borne your guilt and paid the price for you. He descended from the line of Judah. The cross is the central point of your forgiveness; there, your guilt is transferred to Jesus. He will take no money; He wants only your sincere repentance.

God's grace through Jesus Christ is a very special kind of love.

> No-one can understand the message of Scripture who does not
> know the meaning of grace. The God of the Bible is 'the God of
> all grace' (1 Pet. 5:10). Grace is love, but love of a special sort. It
> is love which stoops and sacrifices and serves, love which is kind

to the unkind, and generous to the ungrateful and undeserving. Grace is God's free and unmerited favour loving the unlovable, seeking the fugitive, rescuing the hopeless, and lifting the beggar from the dunghill to make him sit among princes.[50]

Guilt is an invitation to dump your sinful garbage; let Jesus lift you up, and let your guilt become an invitation to receive grace.

The second daughter of Queen Victoria was Princess Alice. At age four, as the story goes, Alice's son was afflicted with black diphtheria, a horrible infection. Doctors quarantined the boy and told the mother to stay away. But one day, she overheard him whisper to the nurse, "Why doesn't my mother kiss me anymore?" His words melted her heart. Princess Alice ran to her son and smothered him with kisses. Within a few days, both were buried.

Through His death on the cross, Jesus smothered you with the kisses of grace. The apostle Paul wrote, "God made him who had no sin to be sin for us, so that in him we might become the righteousness of God" (2 Corinthians 5:21).

Gary Gilmore was a convicted murderer waiting to be executed in Utah. He wrote his girlfriend,

> It seems that I know evil more intimately than I know goodness ... I want to get even, to be made even, whole, my debts paid (whatever it may take!), to have no blemish, no reason to feel guilt or fear ... I'd like to stand in the sight of God. To know that I'm just and right and clean. When you're this way, you know it. And when you're not, you know that too. It's inside all of us, each of us.[51]

We cannot change what's inside us, but Jesus Christ can! We cannot undo our sin, but Jesus Christ, through His loving, voluntary death on the cross, has made sure our sin will not undo us. You can let your guilt become an invitation to receive grace.

A man said to his pastor, "I'm a miserable sinner, and there's no help for me. I've prayed to God, I've tried to be good, and I've tried to do the right thing at the right time, but I always seem to fail."

The pastor asked, "Do you believe in the life, the death, and the resurrection of God's Son Jesus Christ?"

"Yes I do."

"If Jesus came and stood right here beside you at this very moment, what would be your words to Him?"

"I'd look up into His face and confess my sins to Him and then I would tell Him that I feel like a lost sinner and that there is no hope for me."

"What do you think Jesus would say to you?" asked the pastor. The man thought for a few moments. His expression changed from worry to tranquility.

"Jesus would say, 'I have forgiven you of all your sins, you are under no condemnation, you are set free.'"[52]

Let your guilt become an invitation to receive grace.

In Genesis 45, Joseph prepared to reveal himself by saying to his brothers, "Come close to me." Jesus invites you to come close to Him, to come to His cross, to dump your guilt. What greater love can there be than to give one's life? Jesus loves you enough that He died for you, so wed yourself to Christ. Repent of the sin in your life. Take Jesus Christ to have and to hold from this day forward, for better, for worse; for richer, for poorer; in sickness and in health; through time and eternity. Put on His ring of promise: "You are stained red with sin, but I will wash you as clean as snow. Although your stains are deep red, you will be as white as wool" (Isaiah 1:18 GNT). Turn your guilt into grace.

For Your Reflection

And can it be that I should gain
An interest in the Savior's blood?
Died He for me, who caused His pain—
For me, who Him to death pursued?
Amazing love! How can it be,
That Thou, my God, shouldst die for me?'

Tis mystery all: th'Immortal dies:
Who can explore His strange design?
In vain the firstborn seraph tries
To sound the depths of love divine.
'Tis mercy all! Let earth adore,
Let angel minds inquire no more.
'Tis mercy all! Let earth adore;
Let angel minds inquire no more.

He left His Father's throne above
So free, so infinite His grace—
Emptied Himself of all but love,
And bled for Adam's helpless race:
'Tis mercy all, immense and free,
For O my God, it found out me!
'Tis mercy all, immense and free,
For O my God, it found out me!

Long my imprisoned spirit lay,
Fast bound in sin and nature's night;
Thine eye diffused a quickening ray—
I woke, the dungeon flamed with light;
My chains fell off, my heart was free,
I rose, went forth, and followed Thee.
My chains fell off, my heart was free,
I rose, went forth, and followed Thee.

Still the small inward voice I hear,
That whispers all my sins forgiven;
Still the atoning blood is near,
That quenched the wrath of hostile Heaven.
I feel the life His wounds impart;
I feel the Savior in my heart.
I feel the life His wounds impart;
I feel the Savior in my heart.

No condemnation now I dread;
Jesus, and all in Him, is mine;
Alive in Him, my living head,
And clothed in righteousness divine,
Bold I approach th'eternal throne,
And claim the crown, through Christ my own.

Amazing love! How can it be,
That Thou, my God, shouldst die for me?

Charles Wesley, 1738

CHAPTER 8

When the Going Gets Tough ...
The End Becomes the Beginning

Genesis 45:4–16; 46:28–34; 47:1–10

Joseph reveals himself to his brothers

End: a final part of something, especially a period of time, an activity, or a story; a termination of a state or situation; death or ruin.

Many years ago, I read, "Live to learn is good advice, but learn to live is better." I've found that to be wise and true. But how do we learn to live?

We get a cue from Jacob when He was reunited with Joseph. After a long, teary embrace, Jacob said, "Now I am ready to die, since I have seen for myself that you are still alive" (Genesis 46:30). That's powerful stuff.

I had the thrill of portraying Jacob in our church's production of *Joseph and the Amazing Technicolor Dreamcoat*. I was always moved by the reunion scene. I'd limp up the long center aisle, slowly increasing speed with each step. The spotlight would suddenly shine on me, and the audience would anticipate what was going to happen. As the tension mounted, Joseph would turn and spot me. After what seemed like an eternity, Joseph and I would meet in front of the stage and embrace. As I remember this, I get the same goosebumps I got each time we acted that scene. In that small but powerful way, I gained a sense of what led Jacob to utter, "Now I am ready to die." His one last hope for his earthly life had turned into reality. He regained his faith, made wise decisions, and lived a peaceful life. For Jacob, the end became the beginning. Only when we are ready to die, only when we are ready for the end, do we truly learn to live.

Early in the evening, her face glowing with love, a prisoner told her fellow prisoners that though she was engaged to be married, she was ready on this night to meet her heavenly bridegroom.

> For me, this grave is the doorway to a heavenly city. Who can tell the beauty of that city? There, sadness is not known. There is only joy and song. Everyone is dressed in the white of purity. We can see God face-to-face. There are such joys that human language cannot express. Why should I weep? Why should I be sad?

The Communist guards arrived just before midnight. The prisoners quickly gathered around this condemned young Romanian woman, a twenty-year-old who was about to die for her faith in Christ. In the midst of quick whispered good-byes, there were no tears or screams for mercy from her. She stepped toward the approaching guards and recited the Apostles' Creed. Minutes later, the executioners had put an end to her life. Or had they? The reality is they had only sent her to live forever in a much better place.[53]

Only when we are ready to die, only when we are ready for the end, do we truly learn to live. But how do we get ready for the end? These chapters give us at least four guidelines to follow to get ready for the end, and therefore to begin living.

First, we get ready for the end when we accept a Savior.

> Then Joseph said to his brothers, "Come close to me." When they had done so, he said, "I am your brother Joseph, the one you sold into Egypt! And now, do not be distressed and do not be angry with yourselves for selling me here, because it was to save lives that God sent me ahead of you. For two years now there has been famine in the land, and for the next five years there will not be plowing and reaping. But God sent me ahead of you to preserve for you a remnant on earth and to save your lives by a great deliverance. So then, it was not you who sent me here, but God." (45:4–8)

It was necessary for Jacob's family to move to Egypt to be protected, flourish, and grow, but Joseph's brothers' sin had made the road very difficult. Someone had to pay the price to deliver them. That someone was Joseph. His brothers were still guilty, but because of the trials and sufferings of Joseph, they would no longer need to fear God. Catch the truth here: the brothers couldn't undo their sin, but their sin couldn't undo them. Since Joseph paid the price, they were delivered.

How does a good jeweler display a diamond? She puts it on a black velvet cloth; that's the only way to see the diamond's true beauty and cut. Joseph's brothers couldn't see the glory of what God was doing until they could see their deliverer against the backdrop of their sin. It was then they learned that God uses even our sin to accomplish his purposes. As W. M. Taylor wrote,

> God does not need our sin to work out his good intentions, but we give him little other material; and the discovery that through our evil purposes and injurious deeds God has worked out his beneficent will, is certainly not calculated to make us think more lightly of our sins, nor more highly of ourselves.[54]

Have you recognized your deliverer, Jesus Christ? Have you accepted Him as your Savior? Have you placed Jesus Christ against the backdrop of your sin and seen His glory and your forgiveness? Have you firmly grasped the fact that while you cannot undo your sin, your sin cannot undo you? In 1875, Philip Bliss penned some immortal words about Christ.

> "Man of Sorrows," what a name for the Son of God, who came ruined sinners to reclaim! Hallelujah! What a Savior! Bearing shame and scoffing rude, in my place condemned he stood; sealed my pardon with his blood: Hallelujah! What a Savior! Guilty, vile, and helpless, we; spotless Lamb of God was he; full atonement, can it be? Hallelujah! What a Savior!

Are you ready to face Jesus Christ? Or have you found a way to pay for your sin? Until you have accepted Jesus Christ as your Savior, you aren't ready to die, and if you're not ready to die, you're not ready to live. I invite you to accept Jesus Christ as your Savior. It's the only way to the land of refuge; it's the starting point of turning your end into your beginning.

To get ready for the end, you must cooperate with God. In chapter 46, Jacob made sacrifices to and worshipped God at Beersheba. God appeared to assure Jacob of His continued presence and that it was right to go to Egypt—all would be well. From that point on, Jacob was a different person. He walked with God. And that's the definition of cooperate: to act together, to work in combination. Jacob needed that confirmation since he was so hesitant to move on. But then, he realized as never before that God operates and we cooperate. God has His plans and ways.

You can fight Him and be miserable or cooperate with Him and experience His peace. How long has it been since you've offered yourself and your situation to God, since you've submitted everything to Him? Does He guide your decisions about employment, place of residence, relationships, and investments? Do you walk with God?

Martin Buber told the story of a rabbi who one day found several students in the house of study playing checkers rather than studying the Talmud. Embarrassed, they returned immediately to their books. But the rabbi smiled and told them not to be ashamed since they should study the law wherever they found it. He asked if they knew the three rules of checkers. When none responded, the rabbi said, "First, one must not make two moves at once. Second, one may move only forward, not backward. And third, when one has reached the last row, he may move wherever he likes. Such is what the Torah teaches."

Only later did the students grasp what they had been taught—that they should not clutter their lives with more than one move at a time, that they should always keep sight of their goal, and that they would become truly free only as they moved to the last row, making themselves the servants of others. Freedom is discovered in obedience. The secret of living one's life to its fullest is found in submission to the divine rules of play.

Is your surrender partial or full? Is it complete or conditional? Are you content to serve God where you are, or are you always longing for some dream pasture on the other side of the hill? Do you follow Paul's admonition, "Whatever you do, whether in word or deed, do it all in the name of the Lord Jesus, giving thanks to God the Father through him?" (Colossians 3:17). Can you do your daily duty knowing that as your day is, so shall your strength be? Do you really believe that He who began a good work in you will bring it to completion at the day of Jesus Christ? Turn your end into your beginning; submit yourself to the divine rules of play. Get in sync with God. Live His way, obey His mandates, adopt His character, and be at peace. Only when you cooperate with God will you be ready to die, and only then will you be ready to live.

The third guideline for getting ready for the end is that you're ready to die when you have concentrated on your pilgrimage. In response to Pharaoh's question about his age, Jacob said, "The years of my pilgrimage are a hundred and thirty" (Genesis 47:9). Jacob reviewed his life and discovered he never really had had a permanent residence; he realized he was just a journeyman passing through this world. The earth was not the place of his citizenship. Life is not limited to this world or this time. Living is eternal.

> All these people were still living by faith when they died. They did not receive the things promised; they only saw them and welcomed them from a distance, admitting they were foreigners and strangers on earth. People who say such things show that they are looking for a country of their own. If they had been thinking

of the country they had left, they would have had opportunity to return. Instead they were longing for a better country—a heavenly one. Therefore, God is not ashamed to be called their God, for he has prepared a city for them. (Hebrews 11:13–16)

We're prepared to die only when we can look forward to a better land. We're prepared to live only when we recognize there is more to life than this world. As Paul put it, "Our citizenship is in heaven" (Philippians 3:20).

Do you see the picture? As Joseph introduced Jacob to Pharaoh, so Jesus will one day introduce you to the Father. Even now, He's getting ready to welcome you home. As Paul wrote,

> So we fix our eyes not on what is seen, but on what is unseen, since what is seen is temporary, but what is unseen is eternal. Now we know that if the earthly tent we live in is destroyed, we have a building from God, an eternal house in heaven, not built by human hands. Meanwhile we groan, longing to be clothed with our heavenly dwelling ... Now the one who has fashioned us for this very purpose is God, who has given us the Spirit as a deposit, guaranteeing what is to come. (2 Corinthians 4:18ff)

In Genesis 45:14–15, Joseph, upon revealing himself to his brothers, embraced them and wept; afterward, they talked. What a foreshadowing of your future! Perhaps you will see Joseph, but more fantastic, you'll see Jesus Christ and His nail-scarred hands and feet and pierced side. You will realize more powerfully than ever the price He paid, for you will recognize His abundant grace and weep tears of joy! Carrie Breck captured the anticipation so well in what has become a favorite hymn of many:

> Face to face with Christ my Savior, face to face—what will it be when with rapture I behold him, Jesus Christ who died for me? Only faintly now I see him, with the darkening veil between; but a blessed day is coming when his glory shall be seen. What rejoicing in his presence when are banished grief and pain, when the crooked ways are straightened and the dark things shall be plain. Face to face! O blissful moment! Face to

face— to see and know; Face to face with my Redeemer, Jesus Christ who loves me so.

Your pilgrimage on earth will not always be exciting; it will sometimes be very difficult, but because you know your destination, you'll know the journey is worth it. Paul said, "I consider that our present sufferings are not worth comparing with the glory that will be revealed in us" (Romans 8:18).

When my wife and I were engaged, we were separated for a time because of my schooling. My trips from college to where she lived were seldom exciting. Flying standby to one place while my luggage flew somewhere else was tough, and so was traveling on overfilled trains during holidays. But because I knew where I was headed and whom I was going to see, it was always worth the trip! Only if you have concentrated on your pilgrimage in this life, preparing to meet Jesus Christ, will you be ready to die, and only then will you turn your end into a beginning.

Genesis 47:9 also introduces us to the fourth guideline. Jacob continued: "The years of my pilgrimage are a hundred and thirty. My years have been few and difficult, and they do not equal the years of the pilgrimage of my fathers." You'll be ready to die only when you have dealt with brevity. One of those great *Peanuts* cartoons shows Charley Brown and Linus talking. One says, "Life is a lot like a baseball game. We all have certain positions that we play. We all make a few hits and we all make a few errors." The other queries, "How many innings are we playing?" Isn't that the important question? How many innings are you playing? How long do you have to live? Only God knows.

Jacob reported that his life was much briefer than those of his ancestors. Scripture repeatedly teaches the uncertainty and brevity of life. Regarding the uncertainty of life, consider Proverbs 27:1: "Do not boast about tomorrow, for you do not know what a day may bring." Ecclesiastes 6:12 reads, "For who knows what is good for a person in life, during the few and meaningless days they pass through like a shadow?" What security is there in a shadow? Can you hold it? Control it? Determine its size? Can you always count on it being there? So it is with life. Can you hold life in your hands? Control it? Determine its length? Can you always count on it turning out the way you want or plan? Shadows and life are elusive, unpredictable.

Consider Isaiah's picture: "Like a weaver I have rolled up my life, and he has cut me off from the loom" (Isaiah 38:12). Who knows when the weaver will cut the threads? Since your life is being woven by another, you don't get to determine when the threads of life will be cut.

Isaiah points to still another picture: "All people are like grass, and all their faithfulness is like the flowers of the field. The grass withers and the flowers fall, because the breath of the LORD blows on them. Surely the people are grass" (40:6–7). Grass and flowers bloom only for a season. When the Creator breathes on them, it's over. Scripture also points to the brevity of life: "My days are swifter than a runner; they fly away without a glimpse of joy. They skim past like boats of papyrus, like eagles swooping down on their prey" (Job 9:25–26).

What poignant pictures. Swifter than a runner! Have you ever tried to keep up with a sprinter? Our days move by faster than that. Like fast boats skimming over the water. It says, "ships of desire," ships heading home at full speed and leaving a wake. Life is swifter. The winds of time blow by; they never stop. All you can do is ride the wake and try to keep up. The eagle after its prey. An eagle can carry its prey high above the earth, drop it, and catch it before it hits earth; that takes incalculable speed. Yet, says Job, such is life—it flies and swoops swiftly toward its end.

James 4:14 carries on the theme: "You are a mist that appears for a little while and then vanishes." Have you ever seen the mist over a lake on a hazy morning? So thick, yet it's quickly burned away by the sun. It's like blowing bubbles that can be so big and beautiful but burst suddenly and are gone.

But isn't our life expectancy on the rise? Don't new medicine and technology provide for longer lives? Perhaps, but statistics are only averages; they say nothing about individuals. Who's to say the next tragic news headline won't involve you? I still recall that one morning when I was in third grade. My folks kissed my fifteen-year-old sister good-bye as she left for school, never realizing it would be the last time they would do so. Who was to know that a driver late for work wouldn't see her crossing the street and hit her? I still remember the day when as a freshman at college I went into the campus library for the first time, heard a shrill yell, and saw a student athlete fall—an aneurism had burst—and it took his life. You have your stories and reality checks as well. Our lives are not all that secure.

Think about it. As you grow up looking to the future, you buoy yourself with expectations for the future and look ahead to the great American dream of success. As a child, you planned on being a teen; as a teen, you planned on being an adult, as an adult, you planned on being a retiree. You've probably said "Tomorrow!" many times, but how accurately have you predicted everything that happened to you in the past year? One year ago, what were you planning and expecting? Did you count on everything that happened to you? Did your projections and expectations meet the reality of your life?

Life begins when you realize how soon it ends. As Elizabeth Kubler Ross wrote,

> It's only when we truly know and understand that we have a limited time on earth ... and that we have no way of knowing when our time is up ... that we will begin to live each day to the full, as if it were the only one we had.[55]

It's amazing how much we can accomplish when we know our time for some assignment is almost up. If we have certain objectives to meet before we take a vacation, we crank out a great deal of work in the last day or two. When we realize the time for an exam is almost gone, we study furiously. When we see the rain coming, we mow the lawn posthaste.

Since you don't know how long you have to live, take care to do what's most important. Seek first the kingdom of God and His righteousness; make that your top priority. If you're young, you are prone to thinking there's plenty of time to live; don't be fooled—there is no guarantee. If you're middle aged, you know life goes by all too rapidly and won't slow down. If you're in your later years, you know you have no time to lose. No matter your age, remember that life is not a matter of years but of usability. It's never too late to recover the sense of doing the important.

When Napoleon came on the field of Marengo, it was late in the afternoon, and he saw the battle was really lost. But looking at the western sun, he said, "There is just time to recover the day!" Giving out orders with that enthusiasm, he turned defeat into victory.[56]

If you haven't yet begun to serve Christ, start now. If you haven't yet received Jesus Christ as your Savior and Lord, do it now. If you have broken relationships, mend them now. If you know unsaved people, share the gospel now. If people around you are suffering, minister to them now. Remember these words:

> He was going to be all he wanted to be,
> tomorrow.
>
> No one should be kinder and braver than he,
> tomorrow.
>
> A friend who was troubled and weary he knew,
> Who'd be glad of a life and needed it, too,
> On him he would call and see what he could do,
> tomorrow.
>
> The greatest of workers this man would have been,
> tomorrow.
>
> The world would have known him, had he ever seen
> tomorrow.
>
> But in fact he passed on and faded from view,
> And all that he left here when living was through
> Was a mountain of things he intended to do,
> tomorrow.[57]

Have you accepted Jesus Christ as your Savior? Have you been cooperating with God? Are you concentrating on your pilgrimage? Have you dealt with the brevity of your life? If your answer is no to any of these, you're not ready to die—or to live. Your life has not yet begun. The Holy Spirit is waiting to fill you with His overwhelming presence and power. Jesus, like Joseph, says, "Come close to me" so the Holy Spirit can do so.

Once while camping, I tried starting a fire so my family could roast marshmallows, but the wood wouldn't burn. So I doused it with lighter fluid, and the wood immediately lit up. But it soon died out, and the so-called fire smoldered all night. For some reason, the fluid couldn't saturate the wood.

Are you like that wood? You've been touched by the Holy Spirit, maybe even committed your life to Jesus, yet the flame has all but died out and you're only smoldering right now. Life isn't what you hoped it would be or know it could be. Pray right now. Ask the Holy Spirit to knock away all that stands between you and Jesus. Sincerely tell Him you are opening your heart, that you want to be made ready for your end, that you're ready to submit without reserve and willing to do God's will. Your end will be your beginning. You will be ready to live. Do it now; God is waiting. "This is what the Sovereign LORD says to these bones: I will make breath enter you, and you will come to life" (Ezekiel 37:5).

For Your Reflection

> Breathe on me, breath of God,
> Fill me with life anew,
> That I may love what Thou dost love,
> And do what Thou wouldst do.
>
> Breathe on me, breath of God,
> Until my heart is pure,
> Until with Thee I will one will,
> To do and to endure.
>
> Breathe on me, breath of God,
> Blend all my soul with Thine,
> Until this earthly part of me
> Glows with Thy fire divine.
>
> Breathe on me, breath of God,
> So shall I never die,
> But live with Thee the perfect life
> Of Thine eternity.
>
> Edwin Hatch, 1878

CHAPTER 9

When the Going Gets Tough …
Lives Become Legacies

Genesis 47:27–31; 48:15–22; 50:24–26

Jacob prophesies

Lives: plural of life—the period between birth and death of a living thing.

I've presided over 200 funerals. At many of them, people shared good memories of the deceased. But the most moving and memorable funerals were those at which we celebrated a life that left a legacy on which others could build. Have you thought about what you want to leave behind? Do you want to leave mere memories or bestow a living legacy?

After World War I, a great service of praise was held in Royal Albert Hall in London. George Bernard Shaw, the Irish playwright, was seated on the platform next to the pastor of London's City Temple. The huge assembly sang Isaac Watt's hymn "O God, Our Help in Ages Past." When the singing finished, Shaw, deeply moved, said to the pastor, "I'd rather have written that hymn than all of Marx."[58] The missionary William Carey, reflecting on his life and death, said, "When I am gone, speak less of Dr. Carey and more of Dr. Carey's Saviour."[59] Do you want to leave mere memories or bestow a living legacy?

Look in on Jacob and Joseph as they neared the end of their lives. Since both had experienced tough times, their perspectives are valuable. Both gave instructions about what was to happen at and after their deaths; we get a glimpse of how their lives became living legacies. And one vital element of a good legacy is a great faith.

> Jacob lived in Egypt seventeen years, and the years of his life were a hundred and forty-seven. When the time drew near for Israel to die, he called for his son Joseph and said to him, "If I have found favor in your eyes, put your hand under my thigh and promise that you will show me kindness and faithfulness. Do not bury me in Egypt, but when I rest with my fathers, carry me out of Egypt and bury me where they are buried." (Genesis 47:29–30)

Jacob's burial request was not so much sentimental as it was faithful. Canaan was the land God had promised Jacob; His request for burial there showed his faith in God's promises and his interest in the things of God. When Joseph was nearing death, he made the same request of his sons. They were more interested in the things of God than in the things of the world. Perhaps they were the inspiration for Paul's admonition, "Set your minds on things above, not on earthly things" (Colossians 3:2). Bishop James Pike pointed out that when a man says, "I believe in my wife," he's saying something quite different from "I believe I have a wife." The latter is verifiable fact while the first is confirmation he has cast his lot with her. Others need to see you have cast your lot with God, that your faith led you to bet your life on Him so they too will cast their lot with Him no matter what.

Notice as well Jacob's faith blessing.

> Then Joseph swore (the oath) to (his father), and (Jacob) worshiped as he leaned on the top of his staff. (Genesis 47:31)

> May the God before whom my fathers Abraham and Isaac walked faithfully, the God who has been my shepherd all my life to this day, the Angel who has delivered me from all harm - may he bless these boys. (Genesis 48:15–16)

Jacob was doing more than lecturing about God; he was passing on his experience of God. As he leaned on his staff, he recalled the mercies that had molded his life—the heavenly stairs at Bethel, the long working out of God's will with Laban, and the wrestling with the angel that left him with a permanent limp. Jacob recognized that personal experience with God was the most important factor in the development of a godly life. Jacob admitted that whether or not he always followed God, he was constantly led and fed by God, and God led him in a straight line. Jacob might have traveled like a playful dog, turning aside to sniff and sometimes running ahead, but his God always stayed with him and brought him through. So when he blessed Joseph, Jacob called God his shepherd, the first time that name for God had been used. Jacob wanted his descendants to experience the faithful God who cared for them; he wanted to be sure they never lost sight of this God. To bestow a living legacy, you must leave something inside others. Jacob was planting faith in his sons.

There's an old story about two brothers who had been notorious rascals from the cradle. Whenever anything out of line happened around town, they caught the blame, and usually rightly so. After a fire at the school, the boys' parents, driven to the point of distraction, decided they would send the older boy, age ten, to counsel with their pastor. The boy was frightened. The minister looked so austere in his black robe each Sunday. *What will he be like one on one?* the boy wondered. The minister looked somberly at the young boy and asked, "Young man, where is God?" The boy had no idea what to say. The minister asked again, "Young man, where is God?" Still the boy said nothing. So the pastor thundered a third time, "Young man, I asked, where is God?" The boy bolted from the office, raced home, and started packing. He told his younger brother, "You better pack too. They've lost God and they're gonna blame us!" Jacob wanted to be sure his descendants didn't lose God, so he shared his experience, his story of God with them (Genesis 48:1–7).

Who's heard your story? Who needs to? With whom have you shared your experience of God? There was a time when I believed I didn't have a personal story to tell, but thanks to many loving saints, I finally recognized that all God's dealings with me, all His actions in my life, were unique because I was unique. There's no one else like me, so there's no other story like mine. My life might not be a headline grabber or super exciting, but it's mine, and it's written by God, so it's as important as anyone else's.

Since no one else has your story, there's no substitute for it. And those you love have their unique stories as well. Think about how you pray for those you love. Do you pray for them to be free from danger and difficult situations? That's certainly okay. But is it not also wise to pray that whatever their circumstance in life, they would experience God? That no matter what, they'll gain the knowledge that God goes with them to feed and lead them? That when their inheritances are gone, their resources depleted, their stocks depreciated, or they're flat on the ground, they'll still have faith and value and share their stories?

Louis Pasteur, the pioneer of immunology, lived at a time when thousands died each year of rabies. Pasteur had worked for years on a vaccine. Just as he was about to begin experimenting on himself, a nine-year-old, Joseph Meister, was bitten by a rabid dog. The boy's mother begged Pasteur to experiment on her son. Pasteur injected Joseph for ten days, and the boy lived. Decades later, of all the things Pasteur could have had etched on his headstone, he asked for three words: Joseph Meister Lived. Our greatest legacy will be those who live eternally because of our efforts. Turn your life into a legacy—deposit a great faith in others.

A second vital element of Jacob's legacy was that he linked his sons to a glorious future: "Then (Jacob) said to Joseph, 'I am about to die, but God will be with you and take you back to the land of your fathers'"

(Genesis 48:21). As Jacob looked into the future, he proclaimed that the future would be as promised. What a great comfort for Joseph; the Promised Land was secure.

Later on, Joseph gave similar encouragement to his children prior to his death (50:24). Jacob and Joseph reminded their descendants they would see the Promised Land. They had learned well from father Abraham as Hebrews 11:9–10 states it: "By faith he made his home in the promised land like a stranger in a foreign country; he lived in tents … For he was looking forward to the city with foundations, whose architect and builder is God." What a legacy! No matter how grim it looked, no matter how far off course the family seemed to be, the Promised Land awaited them. Jesus expanded the concept in Matthew 5:5: "Blessed are the meek, for they will inherit the earth." In John 14:1–3, Jesus said, "In my Father's house are many rooms … I am going there to prepare a place for you."

You too can embrace your future for you too will live in a better land. Whether your body ends up in a cemetery plot, a mausoleum, the arctic snow, or the sea, you have Christ's promise of a new heaven and new earth where "there will be no more death or mourning or crying or pain" (Revelation 21). Paul wrote, "What no eye has seen, what no ear has heard, and what no human mind has conceived—the things God has prepared for those who love him—these are the things God has revealed to us by his Spirit" (1 Corinthians 2:9–10). Through your daily living, pass on this certainty.

Have others, especially your children and grandchildren, heard you express your hope for the glorious future God has in store? Have they seen how it affects you now? Paul shared how it affected him.

> For God, who said, "Let there be light in the darkness," has made this light shine in our hearts so we could know the glory of God that is seen in the face of Jesus Christ. We now have this light shining in our hearts, but we ourselves are like fragile clay jars containing this great treasure. This makes it clear that our great power is from God, not from ourselves. We are pressed on every side by troubles, but we are not crushed. We are perplexed, but not driven to despair. We are hunted down, but never abandoned by God. We get knocked down, but we

are not destroyed. Through suffering, our bodies continue to share in the death of Jesus so that the life of Jesus may also be seen in our bodies. Yes, we live under constant danger of death because we serve Jesus, so that the life of Jesus will be evident in our dying bodies. So we live in the face of death, but this has resulted in eternal life for you.

But we continue to preach because we have the same kind of faith the psalmist had when he said, "I believed in God, so I spoke." We know that God, who raised the Lord Jesus, will also raise us with Jesus and present us to himself together with you. All of this is for your benefit. And as God's grace reaches more and more people, there will be great thanksgiving, and God will receive more and more glory. That is why we never give up. (2 Corinthians 4:6–16 NLT)

Never give up. This is more than just hard-nosed, tough-it-out perseverance. As the NIV translates it, "We do not lose heart." You can remain positive because you know the future is glorious. What a great assurance and legacy to bestow. Turn your life into a legacy by linking others to a glorious future.

From the lips and life of Joseph came a third vital element of a living legacy; he laid a foundation for his family: "Then Joseph said to his brothers, 'I am about to die. But God will surely come to your aid and take you up out of this land'" (Genesis 50:24). What comfort to his beloved brothers as he was about to die! He reminded them that in the midst of all the changes and decays of life, God's presence was the one constant: "God will surely come to your aid." God has always promised His presence and help.

Since Jacob was afraid, God promised to go with him to Egypt. "I am God, the God of your father," he said. "Do not be afraid to go down to Egypt, for I will make you into a great nation there. I will go down to Egypt with you, and I will surely bring you back again. And Joseph's own hand will close your eyes" (Genesis 46:3–4).

Since Moses was reluctant to lead, God promised that He would go with him and would not fail him: "I will be with you. And this will be the sign to you that it is I who have sent you: When you have brought the people out of Egypt, you will worship God on this mountain" (Exodus 3:12).

Since Joshua was succeeding the great Moses, God promised He would be with him and wouldn't fail him: "No one will be able to stand against you all the days of your life. As I was with Moses, so I will be with you; I will never leave you nor forsake you." (Joshua 1:5).

Through Isaiah, God promised the Israelites, "When you pass through the waters, I will be with you; and when you pass through the rivers, they will not sweep over you. For I am the LORD your God, the Holy One of Israel, your Savior" (Isaiah 43:2–3).

Jesus was named "Immanuel, which means, 'God with us'" (Matthew 1:23). When Jesus arose from the dead, He promised His disciples He would be with them to the end of the age. On Pentecost, He poured out His Spirit to dwell in His people. Peter preached, "This is what was spoken by the prophet Joel: 'In the last days, God says, I will pour out my Spirit on all people. Your sons and daughters will prophesy, your young men will see visions, your old men will dream dreams" (Acts 2:16–17).

On the last day, when He comes again, He will dwell with his people.

> Look! God's dwelling place is now among the people, and he will dwell with them. They will be his people, and God himself will be with them and be their God. He will wipe every tear from their eyes. There will be no more death or mourning or crying or pain, for the old order of things has passed away. (Revelation 21:3–4)

God will always be present to help. This doesn't mean life will always be easy. God's constant presence with Jacob and Joseph, the Israelites, and the disciples (most of whom were martyred) didn't equate to no hardship for them. God's presence with Paul didn't equate to no hardship for him—he was repeatedly beaten, whipped, imprisoned, hunted down, and threatened with death. But listen to Paul.

> For I am convinced that neither death nor life, neither angels nor demons, neither the present nor the future, nor any powers,

neither height nor depth, nor anything else in all creation, will
be able to separate us from the love of God that is in Christ
Jesus our Lord. (Romans 8:35–39)

According to *The Voice of the Martyrs*, the soldiers, while violently
attacking some young boys in South Sudan, demanded the boys say,
"Allah is God, and Mohammed is his prophet." The four young boys—the
youngest only five—cried and screamed out for their mothers but refused
to save their lives by repeating the words that would deny their Christian
faith. Some older teenage boys watched in horror as the younger boys
died. They had seen Southern Sudanese killed at the hands of Islamic
fighters before, but this was worse; these four young boys were friends
and relatives. Though the soldiers had earlier tortured these older boys,
despite the horrific pain, none said the words. Fourteen boys and thirteen
girls were abducted that day. The girls, never located, were likely sold as
slaves or concubines in Northern Sudan. All the boys were tortured, but
not one renounced his faith. The next night, the older boys escaped.[60]
God's presence and help is constant.

There comes a time when God's work is complete in us, but note that
His work continues after us. God's provision is consistent; He carries
on through others. There's always a new leader in the wings. Each new
chapter of God's story has its God-appointed replacement for His work.
There was Noah, then Abraham, Isaac, Jacob, Joseph, Moses, Joshua,
Elijah, and Elisha. There were judges, kings, and prophets; there was
Jesus, then the disciples and Stephen, Paul, and Timothy. We are mortal;
God is eternal. "'For my thoughts are not your thoughts, neither are my
ways your ways' declares the Lord. 'As the heavens are higher than the
earth, so are my ways higher than your ways and my thoughts than your
thoughts'" (Isaiah 55:8–9).

Your attitude toward life and yourself can teach future generations
that God buries the workers but carries on the work. It's so easy in today's
workaholic age to be deluded into believing that only you can do the job. *If
I don't do it, who will?* you think. But there's no president, doctor, or preacher
who is irreplaceable; God has someone waiting in the wings. So relax,
enjoy your work and ministry, and do the best you can, but understand

that the work and the plans are greater than you are and God is always ready to replace you. It's not about you, it's about God!

This also means that no work, including yours, is lost. Since God lives on, so does the work. We each contribute to a great edifice of which Christ is the Chief Cornerstone. The sower dies, but the seed brings forth the harvest. Nothing done for God ever comes to nothing. When you leave this earth, your work, ministry, and witness won't be lost. You will die, but God lives. Paul said, "Therefore, my dear brothers and sisters, stand firm. Let nothing move you. Always give yourselves fully to the work of the Lord, because you know that your labor in the Lord is not in vain" (1 Corinthians 15:58). What better creed could you leave for your descendants? What a grand foundation for turning your life into a legacy.

Jacob and Joseph had the luxury of knowing their deaths were fast approaching and could pass on their legacy to those most important to them. You probably don't know when your death will happen; that means you should plan your legacy now.

Mr. Holland's Opus is a movie about a frustrated composer in Portland, Oregon, who takes a job as a high school band teacher in the 1960s. Although diverted from his lifelong goal of achieving critical fame as a classical musician, Glenn Holland (played by Richard Dreyfuss) believes his school job is only temporary. At first, he maintains his determination to write an opus or a concerto by composing at his piano after putting in a full day with his students. But as family demands increase (including the discovery that his infant son is deaf) and the pressures of his job multiply, Mr. Holland recognizes that his dream of leaving a lasting musical legacy is merely that—a dream. At the end of the movie, we find an aged Mr. Holland fighting in vain to keep his job. The board has decided to reduce the operating budget by cutting the music and drama program. No longer a reluctant band teacher, Mr. Holland believes in what he does and passionately defends the role of the arts in public education. What began as a career detour became a thirty-five-year mission of pouring his heart into the lives of young people.

A few days after school has let out for summer vacation, Mr. Holland returns to his classroom to retrieve his belongings. He has taught his final class. With regret and sorrow, he fills a box with artifacts that represent the tools of his trade and memories of many meaningful classes. His wife and son arrive to give him a hand. As they walk down the hall, he hears some noise in the auditorium. Because school is out, he opens the door to see what the commotion is. To his amazement, he sees a capacity audience of former students and teaching colleagues and a banner that reads "Good-bye, Mr. Holland."

Mr. Holland gets a standing ovation while a band comprising past and present students plays songs they learned at his hand. His wife, who was in on the surprise reception, approaches the podium and makes small talk until the master of ceremonies, the governor of Oregon, arrives. The governor is former student whom Mr. Holland had helped to believe in herself during his first year of teaching.

As she addresses the room of well-wishers, she speaks for the hundreds who fill the auditorium.

> Mr. Holland had a profound influence in my life (on a lot of lives, I know), and yet I get the feeling that he considers a great part of his life misspent. Rumor had it he was always working on this symphony of his, and this was going to make him famous and rich (probably both). But Mr. Holland isn't rich and he isn't famous. At least not outside our little town. So it might be easy for him to think himself a failure, but he'd be wrong. Because I think he's achieved a success far beyond riches and fame.

Looking at her former teacher, the governor gestures with a sweeping hand.

> Look around you. There is not a life in this room that you have not touched, and each one of us is a better person because of you. We are your symphony, Mr. Holland. We are the melodies and the notes of your opus. And we are the music of your life.[61]

Have you thought about your life? Have you thought about turning it into your legacy? Are you linking others to a great faith, a glorious future, and a grand foundation? Will your descendants have great memories of and inherit a great legacy from you? Will they be the symphony of your life? Will that symphony sing of Jesus Christ?

For Your Reflection

No one knows the importance of guided steps as much Fanny Crosby, who had lost her sight in infancy through improper medical treatment. This beloved hymn came from her grateful heart after she had received a direct answer to her prayer. One day when she desperately needed five dollars and had no idea where she could obtain it, she followed her usual custom—she began to pray about the matter. A few minutes later, a stranger appeared at her door with the exact amount.

> "I have no way of accounting for this," she said, "except to believe that God put it into the heart of this good man to bring the money. My first thought was that it is so wonderful the way the Lord leads me. I immediately wrote the poem and Dr. Lowry set it to music."

The hymn was first published in 1875.[62]

All the way my Savior leads me;
What have I to ask beside?
Can I doubt His tender mercy,
Who through life has been my guide?
Heav'nly peace, divinest comfort,
Here by faith in Him to dwell!
For I know, whate'er befall me,
Jesus doeth all things well;
For I know, whate'er befall me,
Jesus doeth all things well.

All the way my Savior leads me,
Cheers each winding path I tread;
Gives me grace for every trial,
Feeds me with the living bread.
Though my weary steps may falter,
And my soul athirst may be,
Gushing from the rock before me,
Lo! A spring of joy I see;

Gushing from the rock before me,
Lo! A spring of joy I see.

All the way my Savior leads me
O the fullness of His love!
Perfect rest to me is promised
In my Father's house above.
When my spirit, clothed immortal,
Wings its flight to realms of day
This my song through endless ages—
Jesus led me all the way;
This my song through endless ages—
Jesus led me all the way.

CHAPTER 10

When the Going Gets Tough …
Revenge Becomes Forgiveness

Genesis 50:15–21

Joseph grants forgiveness

*Revenge: the action of inflicting hurt or harm on someone for an injury
or wrong suffered at their hands; the desire to inflict retribution.*

The scene is familiar. With the trial over and the accused found guilty,
it's time for the sentencing. Before the judge pronounces the sentence,
members of the victims' families take the opportunity to approach the

court and share their views and feelings. In a vast majority of the cases, the result is an emotional barrage of hatred and judgment toward the guilty. I won't stand in judgment of those who respond in this way because I've never stood in their shoes. But what's obvious at such moments is that at times, it's hard to forgive.

A husband abuses his wife for years, a parent mistreats her child, a boss treats his employees like dirt, your best friend cheats you out of a job—that's all hard to forgive. You defend someone you believe has been unjustly accused and find out the person is guilty as charged—that's hard to forgive. A coworker falsely accuses you to cover up for something he's done—that's hard to forgive.

Consider Joseph. For over twenty years, he was separated from his family and knew nothing of their health or whereabouts. Those years had been filled with imprisonment and trials. But he suddenly had to make a choice to take revenge or forgive. Sometimes, it's hard to forgive.

There are of course alternatives to forgiveness. Instead of forgiving, you can seek revenge by trying to get even, to balance the scales. That's the history of Joseph's family. From the time his father, Jacob, was in the womb with Esau, the family's story was one of deceit, trickery, and revenge. Jacob stole his brothers blessing, Laban deceived Jacob with Leah and Rachel, Rachel in turn got even with Laban, and Joseph's brothers took out their jealousy on Joseph and deceived their father. Notice the worry of the brothers when Jacob died. "What if Joseph holds a grudge against us and pays us back for all the wrongs we did to him?" (Genesis 50:15). They expected revenge.

Is revenge so bad? Doesn't Scripture say, "An eye for an eye and a tooth for a tooth" (Exodus 21:24)? People try to balance the scales all the time. There's a story about a grizzled old man who was eating at a truck stop when three tough bikers walked in. The first walked up to the old man and pushed his cigarette into the old man's pie, the second spit into the old man's milk, and the third turned over the old man's plate. Without a word, the old man left. Shortly thereafter, one biker said to the waitress, "Not much of a man, was he?" The waitress replied, "Not much of a truck driver either. He just backed over three motorcycles."[63]

It's cute and easy to chuckle, but revenge never evens the score. Instead, it ties all parties to an escalator of retaliation. If everyone lived by the "eye for an eye" principle, who in the world would have any sight left?

Another alternative to forgiveness is to harbor bitterness and let it rule your heart. But bitterness hurts you more than those you hate. A woman who vowed she'd never forget the injury caused by something her in-laws had said would be far more miserable than they were. The husband who secretly prayed that his ex would be miserable would end up far more miserable than she would. No one can stand up indefinitely under the weight of a grudge.

After the Civil War, Robert E. Lee visited a Kentucky woman who took him to the remains of a grand, old tree in front of her house. She bitterly cried that its limbs and trunk had been destroyed by Union artillery. She looked to Lee for a word condemning the North. Lee said, "Cut it down, my dear madam, and forget it."[64]

Bitterness, passive or aggressive hatred, and anger are malignancies that grow and fester, stifle joy, and threaten health. They must be cut out for your own sake. When you fail to forgive, your life is cemented to your past; you're unable to move forward. You turn the control of your life over to your enemy and set yourself up to suffer the consequences of your lack. Nursing resentment is like eating poison and waiting for the other person to keel over.[65] According to counselors Minirth and Meier, resentment is far more responsible for burnout than overwork.[66] You can choose to harbor bitterness, but you will only suffer in doing so.

There's a third alternative to forgiveness: brokenness. You can choose not to forgive and live as a result in broken relationships. Pastors, counselors, psychiatrists—anyone who counsels people—will testify that without forgiveness, healthy relationships aren't possible. Forgiveness is necessary in all healthy human relationships. If your relationships are broken, you are broken physically, emotionally, mentally, and spiritually.

Rev. Walter Everett was broken. It's impossible for me to even imagine the shock he felt when he learned his son had been shot dead by a neighbor, an addict. Over the months following his son's death, he experienced all the emotions associated with such a tragedy, especially crippling anger, all while carrying on his pastoral ministry and duties. Heavily burdened, he would pray for help, but none seemed to come.

Eleven months after committing the murder, Michael Carlucci receiving a plea-bargained sentence and apologized to the Everett family. At that moment, Walter's heart began to change; his prayer for help was being answered. He began to realize he couldn't move on unless he released his anger. One month later, on the one-year anniversary of the shooting, Walter wrote a letter to the imprisoned Michael Carlucci accepting his apology and offering his forgiveness. He invited Carlucci to write back. That led to exchanges of letters, prison visits by Walter, and the building of a relationship. Walter even spoke at Michael's parole hearing. He also officiated at the funerals of Michael's father and wife and at Michael's wedding to his new wife. Michael and Walter are a team that speaks to people about the power of forgiveness.[67]

Nothing so blocks the healing touch of Jesus than a bitter, unforgiving heart. Nothing so brings the healing touch of Jesus than a forgiving heart. Listen to Jesus' words.

> In prayer there is a connection between what God does and what you do. You can't get forgiveness from God, for instance, without also forgiving others. If you refuse to do your part, you cut yourself off from God's part. (Matthew 6:14 MSG)

Not a very pleasant alternative, is it?

If none of the alternatives to forgiveness is good, how can we seriously pursue forgiveness in times when it's hard? We can remember the acts of forgiveness. There are two related acts. There is first the heavenly act of forgiveness. Scripture uses the image of the people of God as being unfaithful spouses and rebellious children. Jesus portrays a wandering prodigal son. Yet the message of Scripture, the core of our faith, is that through the cross of Jesus Christ, no matter what we have done or failed to do, we are forgiven! There is more mercy in God than there is sin in us. Let the testimony of Scripture sink into our hearts and minds.

> Though your sins are like scarlet, they shall be white as snow; though they are red like crimson, they shall be like wool. (Isaiah 1:18)

> With everlasting kindness I will have compassion on you, says the Lord your Redeemer ... I, even I, am he who blots out your transgressions, for my own sake, and remembers your sins no more. (Isaiah 43:25)

I have swept away your offenses like a cloud, your sins like the morning mist. (Isaiah 44:22)

As far as the east is from the west, so far has he removed our transgressions from us. (Psalm 103:12)

While we were still sinners Christ died for us (Romans 5:8)... If we confess our sins, He is faithful and just and will forgive us. (1 John 1:9)

Therefore there is now no condemnation for those who are in Christ Jesus. (Romans 8:1)

He himself bore our sins in his body on the cross, that we might die to sin and live to righteousness. By his wounds you have been healed. (1 Peter 2:24)

Jerome was a priest and scholar who translated the Bible from Greek into Latin. Oral tradition states that near the end of his life, he had a dream in which Christ appeared to him. He was so overwhelmed by the appearance of Christ that he felt he had to give Christ something. So he offered him money, saying, "Here! This is yours." Christ said, "I don't want it." Jerome brought more possessions. Christ said, "I don't want them either." Jerome said, "If there's anything in the world I can give you, tell me what it is. Tell me! What do you want?" Christ looked at him and replied, "Give me your sin! That's what I came for."[68]

If our greatest need had been information, God would have sent an educator. If our greatest need had been technology, God would have sent a scientist. If our greatest need had been money, God would have sent an economist. If our greatest need had been pleasure, God would have sent an entertainer. If our greatest need had been security, God would have sent a bodyguard. If our greatest need had been health, God would have sent a doctor. If our greatest need had been companionship, God would have sent perfect mates. But our greatest need was forgiveness, so God sent a Savior. "You shall call his name Jesus, for He will save his people from their sins" (Matthew 1:21).

As you remember this heavenly act of forgiveness, do two things. First, seek forgiveness. The brothers of Joseph came to him to seek it; granted, it was with great hesitation and deceit, but they knew they needed forgiveness. So you must seek it first from your heavenly Father. You can never sink below the level of God's grace in Christ. When the first Christian missionaries went to Alaska, they couldn't find a word in the native language for "forgiveness." So they compounded one that would make sense to the Eskimos. Here's the word, which makes no sense to us: *issumagijoujungnainermik*.[69] Its profound meaning, however, is "not being able to think about it." That's the essence of forgiveness—it makes no sense outside of God's love. So clean out your heart first; come to Christ for your own forgiveness.

In his book *Will Daylight Come?* Richard Hoefler shared a wonderful story. A little boy was given his first slingshot while visiting his grandparents. He practiced in the woods but could never hit his target. As he came into his grandparents' backyard, he spied Grandma's pet duck. On an impulse, he took aim and let fly. The stone hit, and the duck fell dead. The boy panicked. He hid the dead duck in the woodpile, but he saw his sister had been watching.

After lunch, Grandma said, "Sally, let's wash the dishes." Sally said, "Johnny told me he wanted to help in the kitchen today, didn't you, Johnny?" She whispered to him, "Remember the duck."

Later, Grandpa asked if the children wanted to go fishing. Grandma said, "I'm sorry, but I need Sally to help make supper." Sally smiled. "That's all taken care of. Johnny wants to do it." She whispered to him, "Remember the duck." Johnny stayed while Sally went fishing.

After several days of this blackmail, Johnny finally confessed to Grandma that he had killed the duck. "I know, Johnny," she said, giving him a hug. "I was standing at the window and saw the whole thing. Because I love you, I forgave you. But I wondered how long you'd let Sally make a slave of you."[70]

How long will you let your sin make a slave of you? Seek forgiveness from your Father. God will throw your sins into the sea and put out a sign that reads, No Fishing! Then seek forgiveness from whomever you have offended. Jesus said,

> Therefore, if you are offering your gift at the altar *and there remember that your brother or sister has anything against you,* leave your

gifts there in front of the altar. First go and be reconciled to them; then come and offer your gift. (Matthew 5:21ff; emphasis mine)

I'll never forget one horrid moment. I was conducting a funeral for the father of some dear friends. They were members of our congregation, but their father hadn't been; I had barely known him. I referred to the deceased by the wrong first name. His dear daughter-in-law, my friend, drew my attention and corrected me. I knew the right name, and I know how it happened, but that's unimportant. What's important is that I had seriously erred at a critical moment. Only by grace did I make it through.

The not-so-nice comments directed to me by some of their friends after the service added to my pain. In my embarrassment and humiliation, I knew I had one thing to do as soon as possible after the funeral: seek their forgiveness. I had no doubt God had forgiven me, but without seeking their forgiveness, I couldn't be whole. In doing so, I got more than I deserved. They forgave me and told me to forget it. They'd already moved on.

There's no guarantee human forgiveness will be granted. I was blessed by dear, precious people. But whether they would forgive me wasn't the issue; all I could do was seek it. In that, God would grant me some peace. Seek both divine and human forgiveness. Then with the Spirit's help, you can move to the next act of forgiveness, the human act. Pray for the Holy Spirit to help you forgive those who have offended you. The only way you can move ahead is by dumping the explosive powder of anger and revenge, and you do that by forgiving. Since you might not feel like doing that, realize you can do it only through the Holy Spirit. As John Henry Jowett said, only "the Lord of grace can do it for me. He can change my weather." God can create a new climate in you. That's what David prayed for when he prayed, "Create in me a clean heart, O God, and renew a steadfast spirit within me" (Psalm 51:10).

The closer you walk to divine forgiveness, the more you'll be able to forgive. In verse 19, Joseph responded to his brothers, "Am I in the place of God?" Joseph stopped the vicious cycle of revenge in his family. He chose not to seek revenge, to get even, to hate, to be bitter, to remain broken; he put God and his family above revenge. Who could blame him if he had chosen retribution? But he didn't. The closer you walk to divine forgiveness, the better you'll be able to forgive. Jesus taught us to pray, "Forgive us our debts *as* we forgive our debtors" (emphasis mine). Paul wrote, "Be kind and compassionate to one another, forgiving each other, just as in Christ God forgave you" (Ephesians 4:32). Your capacity to receive forgiveness depends on your willingness to grant it.

Children are often purer and more loving than adults are; so it is with forgiveness. A therapist asked her nine- to fifteen-year-old challenged children, "What is forgiveness?" Here are some responses.

- "It's when my mother screams at me and says she hates me for being a burden, but it's okay, because I know she really loves me, and she's just feeling sad."
- "It's when other kids make fun of me and laugh at me because I can't walk … but instead of being mad, it makes me want to ask God to make them feel good inside so they don't have to laugh at less fortunate people to make themselves feel good."
- "It's when Mommy reminds me every day that Daddy left because he needed to find something he couldn't find here … not because he doesn't love us. Sometimes, I hate Daddy for leaving us, but Mommy says he still loves us, and she prays for him every night."

There are at least three steps to the human act of forgiveness. First, offer forgiveness. Go to the offending person and say, "I forgive you." Philip Yancey wrote of Joseph this way.

> By forgiving one another, I am trusting that God is a better justice-maker than I am. By forgiving, I release my own right to get even and leave all the issues of fairness for God to work out. When Joseph finally came to the place of forgiving his brothers, the hurt did not disappear, but the burden of being their judge fell away. Though wrong does not disappear when I forgive, it loses its grip on me and is taken over by God, who knows what to do. Such a decision involved risk, of course; the risk that God may not deal with the person as I would want.[71]

Offer forgiveness even if there are no guarantees of acceptance.

Mandisa Hundley, gospel singer and one of the twelve finalists one year on the TV show *American Idol*, met with judges Simon Cowell, Paula Abdul, and Randy Jackson to find out if she had made it through to the next round of the competition. Simon had previously made a sarcastic remark on seeing Mandisa, a heavyset woman: "Do we have a bigger stage this year?" When she entered the room to learn the judges' verdict, Mandisa addressed Simon.

> Simon, a lot people want me to say a lot of things to you. But this is what I want to say ... yes, you hurt me, and I cried, and it was painful. It really was, but I want you to know that I've forgiven you, and that you don't need someone to apologize in order to forgive somebody. And I figure that if Jesus could die so that all of my wrongs could be forgiven, I can certainly extend that same grace to you. I just wanted you to know that.

Randy said, "Amen." Simon apologized and hugged the singer, and Mandisa discovered she had been selected to advance to the next round. Offer forgiveness even if there are no guarantees of acceptance.

Second, pray for the offender. Amazing things happen when you pray for others; you cannot pray for someone daily and continue to hold bitterness against them. Hatred and bitterness melt away. Your prayers for them will change you.

Third, do a kindness for the offender. Live out your forgiveness as Joseph did for his brothers. "'So then, don't be afraid. I will provide for you and your children.' And he reassured them and spoke kindly to them" (v. 21). Chris Carrier of Coral Gables, Florida, was abducted in 1974 when he was ten. His kidnapper, angry with the boy's family, burned him with cigarettes, stabbed him numerous times with an ice pick, then shot him in the head and left him to die in the Everglades. Remarkably, the boy survived, though he lost sight in one eye. No one was ever arrested.

Twenty-two years later, David McAllister, a frail, blind, seventy-seven-year-old ex-convict, confessed to the crime. Chris, then a youth pastor, went to see him in his nursing home. Chris began visiting often, reading the Bible to him and praying with him. That opened the door for McAllister to make a profession of faith. Carrier said,

> While many people can't understand how I could forgive David McAllister, from my point of view I couldn't not forgive him. If I'd chosen to hate him all these years, or spent my life looking for revenge, then I wouldn't be the man I am today, the man my wife and children love, the man God has helped me to be.[72]

Do a kindness for the offender.

Forgiveness can be hard; it's never easy, but you always have a choice. You can live in misery and pain while carrying bitterness, brokenness, and hatred to your grave, or you can follow the steps of forgiveness.

The greatest influences in my life in this area of forgiveness other than Jesus were my parents. When my sister was hit by a car on her way to school and killed by a driver in a hurry to get to work on time, my parents refused to press charges. Even in the midst of their pain, they didn't have bitter hearts. I realized again as I wrote this chapter that one of the reasons they were able to die in peace was that their hearts were free of bitterness and hatred. I hope and pray it can be so for me and you. It changes us and those around us. Forgiveness is the fragrance the lavender leaves on the heels of the one who stepped on it.[73]

Make a decision today to be at peace with God, yourself, and others. God stands ready to help, but only you can turn revenge into forgiveness. Only you know what weight you are carrying and what broken relationships exist in your life because of your lack of forgiveness either given or received. May the Spirit of God convict you until you seek forgiveness and seek to forgive others. "You can't get forgiveness from God, for instance, without also forgiving others. If you refuse to do your part, you cut yourself off from God's part." This is serious business. Because forgiveness is hard, remember the act of forgiveness in Jesus Christ. May His life and death create a new climate in you.

For Your Reflection

What is God saying to you at this moment?

What will you do?

Hover o'er me, Holy Spirit,
Bathe my trembling heart and brow;
Fill me with Thy hallowed presence,
Come, O come and fill me now.

Thou canst fill me, gracious Spirit,
Though I cannot tell Thee how;
But I need Thee, greatly need Thee,
Come, O come and fill me now.

I am weakness, full of weakness,
At Thy sacred feet I bow;
Blest, divine, eternal Spirit,
Fill with power and fill me now.

Cleanse and comfort, bless and save me,
Bathe, O bathe my heart and brow;
Thou art comforting and saving,
Thou art sweetly filling now.

Refrain
Fill me now, fill me now,
Jesus, come and fill me now;
Fill me with Thy hallowed presence,
Come, O come, and fill me now.

CHAPTER 11

When the Going Gets Tough …
Discipline Becomes Production

Genesis 45:5–8; 50:15–26

> *Discipline: the practice of training people rules or a code
> of behavior; activity or experience that provides mental
> or physical training; a system of rules of conduct.*

It started with the Tough Man contests; now, it's become a professional but barbaric sport in which people box, kick, and wrestle each other to see who is the toughest and who can survive the longest. People who participate must be in great shape. While I'd never attend one let alone enter one, they do picture the truth that life is sometimes very tough and often feels like a kick-boxing match. And we must be in shape to survive; we cannot be tough one minute and soft the next.

Joseph is a model for us. He graduated with honors from the University of Hard Knocks. This final chapter provides an analysis of the disciplines of his life that made him so tough. His discipline made him productive. Our ability to be tough is directly proportional to our discipline.

Joseph's first discipline was that he lived a life of constant contact. Near the end of his life, Jacob described Joseph as "a fruitful vine near a spring, whose branches climb over a wall" (49:22). Joseph, like a healthy vine, was never out of touch with the source of his life, God. This constant contact was the foundation of his life.

Ladders and I are friends; not great friends, but we get along. Most of the time. I say most of the time because I'm not a great fan of heights.

120

But it's also because if I'm going to accomplish my task up high, I need to have a firm foundation below.

Joseph made sure he had a firm foundation; he stayed in contact with God and was therefore ready for whatever life brought his way. When Potiphar's wife tried to seduce him, he responded, "How can I sin against God?" While in prison, he heard the cupbearer's and the cook's dreams and offered God, not himself, as the interpreter of dreams. When confronting his brothers, who feared revenge from him, he responded, "Am I in the place of God? You intended to harm me, but God intended it for good."

Joseph portrayed the person pictured by the psalmist: "That person is like a tree planted by streams of water, which yields its fruit in season and whose leaf does not whither. Whatever they do prospers" (Psalm 1:3). God is less concerned with how high you climb than He is with how deeply you've dug your roots. He is less concerned with what you could do "if only" than He is with what you're doing for Him where you are. Whether from the foot of a pit or the head of the kingdom, Joseph faced and stayed in contact with God.

Do you tap daily into the well of God's resources? Like a vine, you need, as Charles Spurgeon once said, to penetrate below the soil and reach the secret fountains of grace. Does that describe your walk and commitment? Remember that character is not made in crisis; it's only displayed then. Discipline becomes productive in the tough times of life. Satan's ploy is to keep you shallow, to keep you dependent on some person or system of beliefs, or some other crutch, but none of these is sufficient. The real question is, what would be left if you were cut off from everyone and everything? Would your roots run deep enough into Christ that you could withstand? Whether you survive tough times depends on the state of your discipline. Former heavyweight boxing champion Joe Frazier reportedly said,

> Champions don't become champions in the ring—they are merely recognized there ... You can map out a fight plan or a life plan. But when the action starts, you're down to your reflexes. That's where your road work shows. If you cheated on that in the dark of the morning, you're getting found out now under the bright lights.

Julie Andrews, a wonderful actress and singer, knew the value of discipline as well.

> Some people regard discipline as a chore. For me, it is a kind of order that sets me free to fly.

In the movie *Karate Kid*, young Daniel asks Mister Miagi to teach him karate. He agrees with one condition—Daniel must submit totally to his instruction and never question his methods. Daniel agrees and shows up eager to learn. But Miagi has him paint a fence, demonstrating the precise motion to use; it takes Daniel days to finish the job. Then Mr. Miagi tells him to scrub the deck using a prescribed stroke; again, it takes days to finish the job. Daniel wonders what this has to do with karate but keeps quiet. Next, Mr. Miagi instructs him to wash and wax three weather-beaten cars, again with a prescribed motion. With that, Daniel reaches his limit: "I thought you were going to teach me karate, but all you have done is have me do your unwanted chores!" He's now broken the one condition, and Miagi's face pulses with anger: "I've been teaching you karate! Defend yourself!" He thrusts his arm at Daniel, who instinctively defends himself with an arm motion exactly like that used in one of his chores. Miagi kicks, and same thing happens. Several more times, the same thing happens. Miagi simply walks away, leaving Daniel to discover that skill comes from repeating seemingly mundane but correct actions.

Engaging in the seemingly mundane action of spiritual disciplines as the foundation of your life will set you free to fly; they will develop in you the strength and skill to survive the tough times. Evaluate your daily schedule and activities. How much time do you spend in intentional contact with God through prayer, Bible reading, fasting, or serving? Do you feel your current level is establishing an adequate foundation?

This great foundation in Joseph's life led to tremendous fruitfulness. Joseph didn't make fruit; he put down the roots that grew into fruitful vines. Recall Jesus' words: "I am the vine; you are the branches. If you remain in me and I in you, you will bear much fruit; apart from me you can do nothing" (John 15:5). I appreciate how Eugene Peterson translated it in *The Message*: "I am the Vine, you are the branches. When you're joined with me and I with you, the relation intimate and organic, the harvest is sure to be abundant. Separated, you can't produce a thing." That hits the nail on the head.

My wife and I love to grow sugar peas. We learned early on that for a long time there will be no produce—the vines just get taller and taller. Only when the vines are ready will any blossoms appear. Joseph was so well rooted in God over such a long time that his branches reached out to all who came into contact with him. Whether in slavery, in prison, in the ruler's house, or in the king's court, Joseph touched everyone around. The same can be true in your life.

And that's important because you're known by your fruits. Your life will speak for itself if you're well rooted. A little boy walking down the beach spied a matronly woman sitting under a beach umbrella "Are you a Christian?" he asked her. "Yes." "Do you read your Bible every day?" "Yes." "Do you pray often?" "Yes." The little boy asked, "Will you hold my quarter while I swim?" Your life will speak for itself if you're well rooted.

Jesus said "To have good fruit you must have a healthy tree; if you have a poor tree, you will have bad fruit. A tree is known by the kind of fruit it bears" (Matthew 12:33 GNT). There's a story that the Arab chieftains Lawrence of Arabia brought to the Paris Peace Conference in 1918 were impressed with all the modern conveniences of France, in particular, running water in their hotel rooms. When they prepared to leave Paris, Lawrence found them trying to detach the faucets so they could have running water in their deserts. They didn't understand that faucets not connected to water reservoirs were useless.

Your life is useless in producing fruit unless you're rooted in Christ; fruitfulness flows only from Him. A sign I once saw captures it cleverly and well: "I want to be so full of Christ that if a mosquito bites me it flies away singing, 'There is Power in the Blood!'" Make constant contact with God, the foundation of your life so in tough times your life will produce fruit.

The second discipline of Joseph's life was consistent conduct. When his brothers, following the death of their father, approached him in fear, Joseph reassured them, "Don't be afraid. I will provide for you and you children" (50:21). This response was not a surprise; he acted predictably because he had integrity. His life was complete, whole, unified. He was in reality what he appeared to be. His life had firmness to it.

The National Institute of Standards and Technology (formerly the Bureau of Standards) is in Washington, DC. From the smart electric power grid and electronic health records to atomic clocks, advanced nanomaterials, and computer chips, innumerable products and services rely in some way on technology, measurement, and standards provided by the institute.[74] Everything is measured by an acceptable standard. Joseph measured his life by and was obedient to God's set of standards. He had integrity; he talked the walk and walked the talk.

In 1 Kings 9:4–5, we find a strong example of this kind of firmness and integrity.

> As for you, if you walk before me faithfully with integrity of heart and uprightness, as David your father did, and do all I command and observe my decrees and laws, I will establish your royal throne over Israel forever, as I promised David your father when I said, "You shall never fail to have a successor on the throne of Israel."

God's commandments, decrees, and laws were to be Solomon's standards; only by obeying, by being faithful and living with integrity would Solomon fully experience God's promises.

In the calm days of Roman prosperity, when the rich lived in marble palaces on the banks of the Tiber, there was a kind of competition in building beautiful, artistic dwellings. Good sculptors were sought, but tricks were sometimes practiced then as now. If a sculptor came upon a flaw in the marble or accidentally chipped a piece, he had a carefully prepared wax with which he filled the chink or blemish so it couldn't be noticed. However, over time, heat and dampness revealed the wax. The result was that whenever contracts were made for commissioned works of art, a clause was added which meant "without wax." Is your life without wax?

One Sunday, a pastor preached a sermon on honesty. On Monday, he took the bus to his office. He paid the fare, and the bus driver gave him back too much change. During the rest of the journey, the pastor was rationalizing how God had provided him with some extra money, but he couldn't live with himself, so he returned the money and told the driver,

"You've given me too much change." The driver smiled. "No mistake. I was at your church yesterday and heard you preach on honesty. I decided to put you to a test this morning." The pastor was without wax.

Did you ever have someone say to you, "I knew you'd say that" or "I knew you'd do that"? While it can be frustrating to hear, it's a compliment because it shows your life has stability, firmness, and integrity. Joseph was unswerving in his faith in God and his people; he was never blown away by what happened to him. Temptation couldn't derail him. He interpreted dreams even though they weren't pleasant to report. He forgave his brothers even though he had missed over twenty years of life with his family because of them. During times of pressure, Joseph's character never wavered.

Where are you on the integrity scale? Do your words and actions match up? In England in 1662, thirty Quakers had been thrown into Newgate Prison for refusing to swear by an oath as the law required. They had insisted, "We Quakers make no oaths. Our word is our bond." Their prison was overcrowded, so the warden offered to move the Quakers to another prison. He was however severely short of guards. He told them, "You know the way. Promise me you'll get there before nightfall and I'll be sure you will." They followed their leader, Thomas Elwood, from one prison to another. As Elwood later said, "Our word is our keeper."[75] Where are you on the integrity scale? How firm is your word and life?

When Joseph had a job to do, he did it. As noted in previous chapters,

- He was not just a son—he we was an obedient son.
- He was not just a slave—he was a faithful slave.
- He was not just a prison keeper—he was an honorable prison keeper.
- He was not just a household manager—he was a trusted household manager.
- He was not just a ruler—he was an esteemed ruler.

Whenever, wherever, Joseph was faithful to God by being faithful to his daily assignments. He understood he was not a volunteer choosing what he would and wouldn't do for God. Rather, he was responsible for whatever God assigned him. This distinction between being a volunteer versus being a steward is critical. Volunteers do what they choose when they choose to do it; not so with stewards.

Matthew recorded parables (24:45–25) that deal with being responsible to the task at hand. They all teach us that like Joseph, when you have your job to do, do it. Be faithful. No matter what the cost—rejection, mistreatment, injustice, abandonment—be faithful where God has placed you and to what God has asked you to do. You're not a volunteer but a servant under the management and orders of your Master.

The difficulty is that most of us like to serve more than we desire to be servants because as long as we can choose where we want to serve, we're in charge, and we like it that way. However, if we desire to be servants, we must give up control to our Master, who determines when and where we serve, and that makes us uncomfortable at times. But our consistent conduct, firmness, and faithfulness will be productive.

Do not waver in your beliefs. If you believe nothing comes to you by chance but all passes through your Father's hand, you know your current situation is His appointment with you. If you believe God created you unique (Psalm 139), you'll know He created you uniquely for your situation. If you believe God is faithful, you'll know you can be faithful where you are. If you believe God will never ask you to do anything for which He has not equipped you, you will know you're equipped for anything, anywhere. If you believe you can count on God, you will know God is counting on you. If you believe God has you here and now on purpose, you'll know He has a purpose for you here and now. God does not want someone else here; He wants you. Be faithful where God has placed you; do what God has asked you to do. It's a discipline that will become productive especially when the going gets tough.

To be tough in tough times, maintain contact and be consistent in your conduct. To that, add a third discipline from Joseph's life, one that doesn't deal so much with action as it does with attitude. Joseph believed in a conscious control in his life. Read again these words from Genesis 45:5–7 and 50:20.

And now, do not be distressed and do not be angry with yourselves for selling me here, because it was to save lives that

God sent me ahead of you. For two years now there has been
famine in the land, and for the next five years there will be no
plowing and reaping. But God sent me ahead of you to preserve
for you a remnant on earth and to save your lives by a great
deliverance … You intended to harm me, but God intended
it for good to accomplish what is now being done, the saving
of many lives.

Everything God does is by plan. Do you think it was chance that
there was no water in the pit into which the brothers dumped Joseph?
That the Ishmaelites were traveling to Egypt and came by the pit while
the brothers were there? That Joseph found favor in the eyes of Potiphar?
That Potiphar's wife tried to seduce Joseph? That Joseph was in prison at
the time the cupbearer and baker had their dreams? That the cupbearer
didn't remember Joseph's dream interpretation ability until Pharaoh had
a dream? That Joseph's family experienced a famine that sent them to
Joseph?

Joseph related everything in his life to the overarching plan of God.
God has a plan for the salvation of the world, for your salvation, and for
your participation in that plan. Do not doubt that God always works for
the saving of life. He even used a cross on which his Son was crucified
to bring life! Paul wrote, "And we know that in all things God works for
the good of those who love him, who have been called according to his
purpose" (Romans 8:28).

Jesus' resurrection was God taking charge of your sin and working it
out for your good. Even in the worst of circumstances, God works to bring
forth good and beauty. It's God's chemistry at work. As the old adage goes,
if you eat the ingredients of a cake separately, some of them will not taste
good, but when they're mixed properly and baked just right, they produce
a delicious cake. So with the ingredients of your life. Maybe you've been
betrayed, rejected, and neglected; perhaps you've been misunderstood or
overlooked. It could be that things haven't worked out as you had hoped
or your dreams have fallen apart. You might still be waiting on God to
answer your prayers. Keep your faith. In God's providence, the ingredients
of your life aren't yet mixed and baked according to the Master Chef's
recipe, but He is at work.

No experience is wasted if you release control to God. I still recall a teenage girl who was killed in an auto accident. It was as always very tragic, and the funeral was difficult. Yet after the funeral, one of her friends who had been somewhat wayward recommitted her life to Jesus Christ. In the tragedy, God worked for life, for salvation, for good. He always does even if you cannot see it at the time.

That's why believing this truth leads to trust. Since you know the last word is always God's, you can trust because His last word is never darkness, despair, or death but light, love, and life. This means you must allow for mystery in life, but mystery is okay; you don't need all the answers. Joseph believed his brothers acted freely: "You intended to harm me." Yet he also believed God was in control: "God intended it for good." You could spend your life arguing over who's really in control, God or people. What roles do your character and actions play, and where does God's action and character fit in? Where's the balance between your freedom and God's sovereignty? If you allow for the mystery that both can be true and therefore trust God, you need not settle that issue in this life. If you believe both are true, you'll never think what you do doesn't matter or everything you do depends on you alone.

Lecturing years ago at Calvin Seminary, R. B. Kuiper compared this issue to two ropes going through two holes in the ceiling and over a pulley. We must cling to both ropes if we want support. If we hold totally to God's sovereignty or totally to our free will, we'll fall. Both are necessary. Just trust. If you rid your life of mystery, you rid it of faith; if you rid it of faith, you rid it of Jesus Christ.

The grand old hymn "God Moves in a Mysterious Way" was written by William Cowper (pronounced Cooper). An English poet, a friend of John Newton, Cowper struggled all his life with melancholy. According to Ernest Emurian in *Living Stories of Famous Hymns*, Cowper wrote this hymn following a period of almost suicidal depression. Calling for a carriage, he ordered the driver to take him to the Ouse River three miles away, where he planned to kill himself. The driver, knowing the state of mind of his passenger, breathed a prayer of thanks when a thick fog enveloped the area. He purposely lost his way in the dense fog, jogging up one road and down another as Cowper fell into a deep sleep. Several hours passed as the driver kept going in circles, letting his passenger rest. Finally, he returned him to his home. "We're back home!" said Cowper. "How is that?" "Got lost in the fog, sir. Sorry." Cowper paid his fare, went inside, and pondered how the merciful providence of God had spared him from harming himself. That same evening in 1774, his forty-third year, reflecting on his narrow escape, he wrote this autobiographical hymn.[76]

> God moves in a mysterious way his wonders to perform;
> He plants his footsteps in the sea, and rides upon the storm.
>
> Deep in unfathomable mines of never-failing skill,
> He treasures up his bright designs and works his sovereign will.
>
> You fearful saints, fresh courage take; the clouds you so much dread
> Are big with mercy and shall break in blessings on your head.
>
> Judge not the Lord by feeble sense, but trust him for his grace;
> Behind a frowning providence he hides a smiling face
>
> His purposes will ripen fast, unfolding every hour;
> The bud may have a bitter taste, but sweet will be the flower.
>
> Blind unbelief is sure to err and scan his work in vain:
> God is his own interpreter, and he will make it plain.

Be thankful that God is greater and wiser than you are. Be thankful for His ways, claim the assurance He is with you, in control, and sovereign and yet loves you enough to let you live freely. I love how the psalmist responded to this truth: "Open up before GOD, keep nothing back; he'll do whatever needs to be done: He'll validate your life in the clear light of day and stamp you with approval at high noon" (Psalm 37:5–6 MSG). Your discipline of releasing your life to God's control will produce His approval.

Read this aloud: "There is no one like the God of Jeshurun, who rides across the heavens to help you and on the clouds in his majesty. The eternal God is your refuge, and underneath are the everlasting arms"

(Deuteronomy 33:26–27). How awesome it is to face and endure tough times knowing in whose arms you rest.

During the terrible days of the London blitz, a father led his small son by the hand from a building struck by a bomb. In the front yard was a shell hole. The father jumped into the hole and called up for his son to follow. Terrified, the young boy replied, "I can't see you!" The father, looking up at the sky tinted red by the burning buildings, called to the silhouette of his son, "But I can see you. Jump!" The boy jumped because he trusted his father.

The Christian faith enables you to meet whatever life brings, for in trust, you can always jump into your Father's everlasting arms. Being tough in tough times is not so much a matter of what life brings you but what you bring to life. Bring your faith in Jesus Christ, bring your trust in God, and you'll always be tough in tough times.

Your life can be filled with the recognition of God's faithfulness if your present is filled with a steady faith. You can right now decide to let Jesus into your life at every point, in every moment, in every situation. Let Jesus have control. Let go of whatever you're clasping as your own. Yield to Jesus. Let Him have the right of way in your thoughts, heart, finances, relationships, hobbies, and work. Let Him direct your life.

You are not your own; you belong body and soul, in life and in death, to your faithful Savior, who has paid for your sins with His blood and has freed you from the tyranny of the devil. He also watches over you; not a hair falls from your head without His willing it. All things must work together for your salvation. Because you belong to him, Christ, by his Holy Spirit, assures you of eternal life and makes you wholeheartedly willing and ready from now on to live for Him.[77]

I pray you are ready to let God have the right of way in your life. If so, let Him know. Right now.

For Your Reflection

Make me a captive, Lord, and then I shall be free.
Force me to render up my sword, and I shall conqueror be.
I sink in life's alarms when by myself I stand;
Imprison me within Thine arms, and strong shall be my hand.

My heart is weak and poor until it master find;
It has no spring of action sure, it varies with the wind.
It cannot freely move till Thou has wrought its chain;
Enslave it with Thy matchless love, and deathless it shall
reign.

My power is faint and low till I have learned to serve;
It lacks the needed fire to glow, it lacks the breeze to nerve.
It cannot drive the world until itself be driven;
Its flag can only be unfurled when Thou shalt breathe from
heaven.

My will is not my own till Thou hast made it Thine;
If it would reach a monarch's throne, it must its crown resign.
It only stands unbent amid the clashing strife,
When on Thy bosom it has leant, and found in Thee its life.[78]

Epilogue

There's an appropriate, delightful fable from French fabulist and Poet Jen de La Fontaine called "The Acorn and the Pumpkin." One day, a man was walking through the woods, praying and meditating on the goodness of God. He looked up and saw a tiny acorn on top of a huge oak tree. Then he looked down and saw a thin stem at the end of which was a big pumpkin. The man looked up and he looked down, and he thought, *This is stupid! Too bad I wasn't around at the creation of the world. I would have said, "God, that little acorn should go with that tiny stem, and that big pumpkin should be on that big tree."*

The man decided to sleep under the tree. As fate would have it, the tiny acorn fell off the tree and hit the man on the nose, waking him up and causing him to cry out in pain. Then he realized something. *Suppose things were the way I wanted them. Suppose the pumpkin had been up there!* The man walked away with greater faith in God, saying to himself, *Whatever God does, God does well.*

Appendix

While this book contains numerous illustrations of people who have used tough times as launching pads, having turned their stumbling blocks into stepping stones, I want to draw special attention to one group of people. 3 of the stories are from *The Voice of the Martyrs*.

The Voice of the Martyrs is a non-profit, inter-denominational Christian organization dedicated to assisting our persecuted family worldwide.

Their mission is *"Serving persecuted Christians through practical and spiritual assistance and leading other members of the Body of Christ into fellowship with them."*

Compared to the stories and experiences of our persecuted brothers and sisters around the world, my tough times are not even bumps in the road. The amount of persecution occurring daily is staggering. I have been a supporter and promoter of VOM for many years. I am convinced that their stories must be heard and their cause taken up by those of us who are so richly blessed. If you are familiar with VOM, I challenge you to pray for them and find a way for you – and your congregation – to be involved. If you are not familiar, I have included the link to their website below; I invite and urge you to check out VOM and see how the Lord leads you.

Thank you.

www.persecution.com/public/aboutVOM.aspx

Group Study Questions

Chapter 1

1. Read Genesis 37:1–36

2. Share one of your dreams or plans that collapsed, met with detours, or fell flat.
   - What happened?
   - How did you feel?
   - What did you do?

3. Consider a purpose for your life.
   - Do you have one? What is it? How does it influence you?
   - If you don't have or know a purpose for your life, how is that influencing you? Are you seeking one? If yes, how?
   - How can you determine if it's God's plan for you? How do you know if a dream is God-given?

4. Talk about your relationship with Jesus.

5. Share a tough time in your life.
   - Discuss what you've learned and how you've grown through it.

6. How do you understand and define God's providence? Sovereignty?
   - Where have you seen God's providence and sovereignty in your life?

7. How and where is God calling you to trust Him?

8. How can your group pray for you between now and the next meeting?

Chapter 2

1. Read Genesis 39:1–6.

2. Share a time you were trapped in a pit with no way out, when you were
   - boxed in
   - stymied
   - held hostage

3. What has proven to be a zigzag path in your life?

4. When do you find it hard to accept your situation or circumstance?

5. In your current situation (good or tough), how can you serve God more faithfully?

6. Share a time when you came to know God more clearly or deeply because someone was faithful.

7. Share a time when you experienced God's presence and supply.

8. What would taking hold of Jesus' hand look like for you?

9. What would it mean for you to keep writing your story in your current situation?

10. How can your group pray for you between now and the next meeting?

Chapter 3

1. Read Genesis 39:6–23.

2. What are some names by which Satan, the tempter, is described in the Bible?

3. Do you know someone who yielded to temptation?
    *   What were the results?

4. Share a temptation with which you struggled. What happened?
    *   Did you yield? What was the result?
    *   Did you withstand? What gave you strength to do so?

5. What is one of your Achilles heels?

6. Is there a struggle in your life that helps you identify with Paul in Romans 7? If so, what is it?

7. Where in your life right now do you need to do right?

8. What Scripture verse have you found helpful during times of temptation?

9. How can you turn a current temptation into a testimony?

10. What would "looking into your Master's face" look like for you?

11. How can your group pray for you between now and the next meeting?

Chapter 4

1. Read Genesis 40:1–23.

2. Share a time when you experienced rejection and a time when being nice didn't seem to pay.

3. Describe a time when you were filled with bitterness.
   • Why do you think you felt bitter?
   • How did you get rid of the bitterness?

4. Recount an experience of yours or someone you know when rejection was turned into an opportunity.

5. Tell of an experience when you knew beyond a doubt that it was not chance but God at work.

6. Have you ever missed the presence of God because you were looking at the fog and not the light? Share what happened.

7. Recall a time when you felt God was right there with you.

8. What currently in your life is an appointment with God? What would partnering with God in it look like?

9. How can your group pray for you between now and the next meeting?

Chapter 5

1. Read Genesis 41:1–46.

2. If you know or have visited someone in prison, what have you learned about imprisonment?

3. Recall a time when you felt locked in, restrained against your will, not free to do, or go where you want.

4. Share a time or incident when you wanted desperately to be in control.

5. Why is it so hard to submit?
    *   Is there some area or incident in your life right now you need to submit to God? What is it?

6. On a scale of one to ten, where do you rank yourself in patience?

7. What is God currently teaching you?

8. Discuss a time when you were a buzzard or a bee, a time when you kept your sights so low that you failed to see the upper horizon where God was waiting for you to take notice of Him.

9. Talk about a time when you could see or understand something that others could not.

10. How are you preparing yourself for promotion?
    *   What higher aspirations might God have for you? Ask the group to share their thoughts on this question for you.

11. How can your group pray for you between now and the next meeting?

Chapter 6

1. Read Genesis 42:1–38.

2. Relate an experience when you experienced self-pity.

3. Have you or someone you know ever become numb to sin? What was it like?

4. Share a time when you felt prone to inaction.
   - What was going on?
   - Was it the result of some sin?
   - What did you do?

5. What intersection, what scene, what place, what experience, what journey would be difficult for you to revisit?
   - What is it that try as you will you cannot forget?
   - What are you doing about it?

6. Recall a memory of awaiting "punishment."
   - What did you feel like?

7. Share a time when you became aware of guilt blocking grace in your life or someone else's.
   - What impact did it have on you or that person?

8. Have you ever felt God was punishing you for something you did?
   - What had you done, and how did you feel God was punishing you?
   - Were you ever the victim of your own evil actions, your sin, in some other way?

9. Have you ever viewed God more as a judge than a grace giver?
   - When? Why?
   - Did anything change your view?
   - Was God in fact doing something good or beneficial? What?

10. Share a time when fear stifled you.
    - How did it impact you?

11. Share a time when you knew beyond a doubt that the Lord was "at hand."

12. Tell about a time when you chose to walk by faith, not by sight.

13. Have you ever judged something before its time? Explain.

14. Discuss a time when you were more focused on what you didn't have rather than on what or Whom you had.
    • Is there something in your life currently for which you need to express more gratitude?

15. Is there a current situation in your life where you need to turn pity into profession?
    • What is it?
    • What do you need to do?

16. Where do you need to trust God more for your future?
    • What would that look like?

17. How can your group pray for you between now and the next meeting?

Chapter 7

1. Read Genesis 43:1–44:34.

2. Share a time when you experienced false guilt.
    • How did you feel?
    • When did you realize it was false guilt?

3. Relate a time when you experienced real guilt.
    • How did you feel?
    • When did you realize it was false guilt?

4. Tell of observing someone who was trying to buy forgiveness.
    • What were they doing?
    • What happened?
    • Have you ever tried to do so? How? What happened?

5. Talk about a time when you found repentance difficult.
   - Why was it difficult?
   - When you did repent, what did you repentance look like? What did you do?

6. From your life or that of someone you know, share an experience of "shooting the source" of sin.

7. For what "week" or experience do you still need forgiveness?

8. When have you experienced the "kisses" of Jesus' grace directly from God or through someone else?

9. How can your group pray for you between now and the next meeting?

Chapter 8

1. Read Genesis 45:4–16, 46:28–34, 47:1–10.

2. Share an experience when you or someone you know found new life after confronting death.

3. Has God ever worked His will through your sin or injurious deeds? Explain.

4. Describe a time when you felt God's forgiveness in a powerful way.

5. Tell about a time when you "cooperated" with God. How did you feel?

6. Is there an area of your life in which you need to submit to the divine rules of play? What is it?

7. Share a time when you longed for a dream pasture on the other side of the hill.

8. What experience in your life or in the life of an acquaintance made you acutely aware of the uncertainty and brevity of life?

9. What are some things that have happened in the past year you had not expected or planned on?

10. Discuss a time when you accomplished a great deal in a short amount of time. Why did you do so?

11. What would it look like for you to come close to Jesus?

12. How can your group pray for you between now and the next meeting?

Chapter 9

1. Read Genesis 47:27–31, 48:15–22, 50:24–26.

2. How will others know you have cast your life with God? What evidence is there?

3. Where in your life have you seen God at work leading, guiding, and shepherding you?
    *   When has He come to your aid?

4. What promises of God's constant presence and consistent provision are especially meaningful for you? Why?

5. Whose life story has influenced you?

6. Who has heard your life story?
    *   Share your life story with your group.

7. How and what do you pray for those you love?

8. How do you envision your glorious future?
   - With whom have you shared it?
   - How does knowing your glorious future impact your life?

9. Share a time when you needed to admit that it was about God and not you.

10. If you could title the symphony of your life, what would it be?

11. How can your group pray for you between now and the next meeting?

Chapter 10

1. Read Genesis 50:15–21.

2. Share a time when you found it hard to forgive.
   - What did it feel like?
   - What did you do?

3. Why do you think it is sometimes so hard to forgive?

4. When was a time when you found it hard to seek forgiveness?
   - From God
   - From another person
   - Why was it hard?

5. Tell about a time when you felt like seeking revenge or someone sought revenge on you.

6. Describe a relationship you know that is broken by lack of forgiveness; it could be one of yours or one of a friend or relative. Please safeguard the confidentiality of those others might talk about.

7. When was a time when you allowed your sin to make a slave of you?

8. How do you understand and explain the phrase in the Lord's Prayer, "Forgive us our debts as we forgive our debtors"?

9. Talk about a time when you prayed for another whom you were having trouble forgiving.
   • What happened?

10. What have you learned from this chapter?

11. How can your group pray for you between now and the next meeting?

Chapter 11

1. Read Genesis 45:5–8 and 50:15–26

2. Why is a vine a good image of Joseph's life? What does it communicate?

3. On a scale of one to ten (one being low and ten being high), where do you rank yourself on practicing spiritual disciplines?
   • Why?
   • What changes if any would you like to make?

4. How do you stay in contact with God and keep your face toward Him?

5. Where in your life do you need to measure up more accurately to God's standards?
   • What will it take for you to do so?

6. On a scale of one to ten, where are you on the integrity scale?
   • Why did you choose that ranking?

7. Read and share observations from Matthew 24:45–25:46.
   • Discuss the differences you see between a volunteer and a steward.
   • What takeaways are there for your life right now?

8. Share an illustration or experience of God's providence from your life.

9. Tell of a time you knew you were resting in God's everlasting arms.

10. What do you need to release to God? Explain.

11. What would it mean for you to jump into your Father's arms with complete trust? What is holding you back? What would it take for you to jump?

12. Share any final thoughts or learnings from your study of Joseph.

13. How can your group continue to pray for you?

Notes

1. Scott Larson, *A Place for Skeptics* (Grand Rapids: Bethany House Publishers, 2005).
2. Charles Murray, as quoted in "Gaining Ground," *WORLD* 1 (January 10, 2004): 24–26.
3. Horace Bushnell, *Sermons for the New Life,* (New York: Charles Scribner 1858), 10–11.
4. Nick Vujicic, *Limitless* (Colorado Springs: Waterbrook, 2013), 147–48.
5. Dr. Norman Vincent Peale, *What to Do for a Great New Year* as published in *Creative Help for Daily Living* (Pawling: Foundation for Christian Living, November–December 1982).
6. *The Westminster Collection of Christian Quotations* (Louisville: Westminster John Know Press, 2001)
7. Bruce G. Epperly and Katherine Gould Epperly, *Tending to the Holy—The Practice of the Presence of God in Ministry* (Durham: Alban Institute, 2009), 6.
8. Larson, ibid.
9. Words by Katharina von Schlegel.
10. Author unknown.
11. The comparison between these two news accounts was suggested in *Say Yes to Life: A Book of thoughts for Better Living*, Rabbi Sidney Greenberg (Northvale, NJ: Jason Aronson, Jerusalem), 85.
12. www.coachwooden.com.
13. Author unknown.
14. Leslie T. Lyall. *A Passion for the Impossible: The Continuing Story of the Mission Hudson Taylor Began.* London: OMF Books, 1965) 37.
15. Complete story in Carl Lawrence, *The Church in China* (Bloomington, MN: Bethany House, 1985).
16. Ira F. Stanphil, *I Know Who Holds Tomorrow,* Copyright 1950, New Spring Publishing, ASCAP (CapitalCMGPPublishing.com) All rights reserved. Used by permission.
17. Ibid.
18. The final lines of *Wisegal* on LIFETIME.
19. Lords' Day 52, Q&A #127 (2011 version).
20. John Henry Jowett, *Springs of Living Water* (Grand Rapids, MI: Baker Book House, 1976), February 18/page 49

[21] Dietrich Bonhoeffer, *Temptation* (New York, Macmillan, Collier Books, 1953), 116–17.

[22] *Bits and Pieces*, June 1990, 5-7 (from Bible.org)

[23] Clarence Edward Macartney, *Trials of Great Men of the Bible*, (Nashville, Abingdon Press, 1946), 46–47.

[24] P. L. Tan, *Encyclopedia of 7700 Illustrations: Signs of the Times* (Garland, TX: Bible Communications, 1996), 1447–48.

[25] Greg Laurie, *Lies We Tell Ourselves* (Ventura, Regal, 2006), 99–100, as quoted in the July 19 entry of *Men of Integrity* (July–August 2009).

[26] R. J. Morgan, *Nelson's complete book of stories, illustrations, and quotes*, electronic edition, 725 (Nashville: Thomas Nelson, 2000).

[27] Heidelberg Catechism, Lords' Day 1, Q&A no. 1.

[28] From *Sword of the Lord* as quoted in Tan, *Encyclopedia of 7700 Illustrations: Signs of the Times* (Garland, TX: Bible Communications, 1996), 1444.

[29] Helen H. Lemmel.

[30] *Epistle of Mathetes to Diognetus* (www.earlychristianwritings.com/diognetus.html).

[31] Lords' Day 9, Q&A no.27.

[32] Lenya Heitzig, *Holy Moments: Recognizing God's Fingerprints on Your Life* (Delight, Gospel Light, 2006 - Digitized by Google Books), 61.

[33] Philip Yancey, *Where Is God When It Hurts?* (Grand Rapids, MI: Zondervan, 1977), 95.

[34] Eric Metaxas, *Bonhoeffer: Pastor, Martyr, Spy* (Nashville, Thomas Nelson, 2010), 528.

[35] William M. Taylor, *Joseph: The Prime Minister* (New York: Harper & Brothers, 1886), 74.

[36] Anonymous.

[37] By Karolina W. Sandell-Berg, translated into English by Andrew L. Skoog.

[38] From *Extreme Devotion*, (The Voice of the Martyrs – see Appendix).

[39] Vance Havner, *Consider Jesus* (Grand Rapids, MI: Baker Book House, 1987), 51.

[40] Joseph Bayly, *The Last Thing We Talk About*, formerly published as *The View from a Hearse*, (Colorado Springs: David C. Cook, 1973), 120–21.

[41] Dr. George Sweeting, *Special Sermons for Special Days: Eighteen Condensed Sermons for the Twentieth Century* (Chicago: Moody Press, 1977), 59.

[42] Matthew Henry, *Matthew Henry's Commentary on the Whole Bible: Complete and Unabridged in One Volume* (Peabody: Hendrickson, 1996), Genesis 42:21 LOGOS Bible Software Edition

[43] From *Charisma News*, January 15, 2016.

[44] Lord's Day 10, Q&A no. 28

[45] Copyright 2006 Universal Music, Brentwood Benson Songs, BMI (CapitolCMGPublishing.com). All rights reserved. Used by permission.

[46] Cathleen Crowell Webb, "Trying to Make It Right," www.people.com.

[47] "Washing Your Hands of Guilt," *The Week*, September 20, 2006.

[48] Michael P. Green, ed., *Illustrations for Biblical Preaching* (Grand Rapids, MI: Baker Book House, 1989), no. 627.

[49] Jean-Paul Sartre, *No Exit and Three Other Plays* (New York, Vintage Books, 1949), 72.

[50] From *Understanding the Bible* (rev. ed. London: Scripture Union, 1984), 127; excerpted from *Authentic Christianity*, InterVarsity Press, 181.

[51] *Illustrations for Biblical Preaching*, no. 626.

[52] From a sermon by Bill Butsko, "Set Free," July 27, 2008, www.sermoncentral.com/sermon.asp?SermonID=124974.

[53] From *Extreme Devotion*, (The Voice of the Martyrs – see Appendix).

[54] W. M. Taylor, *Joseph—The Prime-Minister* (New York: Harper & Brothers, 1904), 138.

[55] From Robert Atwell, *Soul Unfinished* (Brewster, MA: Paraclete Press, 2012), 122.

[56] Taylor, 151.

[57] Edgar Guest.

[58] *The World Tomorrow*, Vol. IV No. 8, *Ex Libris*, p. 254 ebook edition)

[59] P. L. Tan, *Encyclopedia of 7700 Illustrations: Signs of the Times* (Garland, TX: Bible Communications, 1996), 314.

[60] From *Extreme Faith*, (The Voice of the Martyrs – see Appendix).

[61] *Mr. Holland's Opus* (Hollywood Pictures, 1995); rated PG.

[62] K. W. Osbeck, *Amazing Grace: 366 Inspiring Hymn Stories for Daily Devotions* (Grand Rapids, MI: Kregel, 1996), 259.

[63] *Preaching Now*, January 22, 2008.

[64] Charles Bracelen, *Lee: The Last Years* (Boston, Mariner Books 1998), 152.

[65] Anonymous, from Robert Atwell, *Soul Unfinished* (Brewster, MA: Paraclete Press, 2012), 72.

[66] R. J. Morgan, *Nelson's complete book of stories, illustrations, and quotes*, (electronic edition, 314 (Nashville: Thomas Nelson, 2000).

[67] News stories in the *Hartford Courant*, September 20, 1993; November 13, 1994; September 25, 2014.

[68] Cited in blog of Ijboudreaux.com/tag/st-jerome, July 15, 2014; *Give Me Your Sins*.

[69] John MacArthur, *New Testament Four Volume Set*, Matthew 1-28 (Chicago, Moody Publishers, 2004) online edition Matthew 9:2b

[70] Craig Brian Larson, *Illustrations for Preaching and Teaching* (Grand Rapids: Baker Books, 1993), 89.

[71] Yancey, 93.

[72] From numerous newspaper accounts.

[73] Attributed to Mark Twain.

[74] www.nist.gov/public_affairs/general_information.cfm.

[75] Thomas Elwood, *The History of the Life of Thomas Elwood*, (Headley Brothers, 1906 - Digitized by Google Books), 158.

76 R. J. Morgan, *Nelson's complete book of stories, illustrations, and quotes*, electronic ed., 652–53 (Nashville: Thomas Nelson, 2000).

77 Answer no. 1, Heidelberg Catechism.

78 "Make Me a Captive, Lord," George Matheson, *Sacred Songs*, 1890.